WHAT THEY DIDN'T TEACH YOU IN GRADUATE SCHOOL 2.0

WHAT THEY DIDN'T TEACH YOU IN GRADUATE SCHOOL

2.0

299 Helpful Hints for Success in Your Academic Career

PAUL GRAY and DAVID E. DREW

Foreword by *Laurie Richlin*
Foreword by *Steadman Upham*
Cartoons by *Matthew Henry Hall*

STERLING, VIRGINIA

Published by Stylus Publishing, LLC
22883 Quicksilver Drive
Sterling, Virginia 20166-2102

Library of Congress Cataloging-in-Publication Data
Gray, Paul, 1930–
    What they didn't teach you in graduate school : 299 helpful hints for success in your academic career / Paul Gray and David E. Drew ; foreword by Laurie Richlin, Steadman Upham.—2nd ed.
        p.   cm.
    Includes bibliographical references.
    ISBN 978-1-57922-643-5 (cloth : alk. paper)
    ISBN 978-1-57922-644-2 (pbk. : alk. paper)
    ISBN 978-1-57922-645-9 (library networkable e-edition)
    ISBN 978-1-57922-646-6 (consumer e-edition)
    1. College teaching—Vocational guidance—United States.   2. College teachers—United States.   3. First year teachers—United States.   I. Drew, David E.   II. Title.
    LB1778.2.G73   2012
    378.1′202373—dc23
                                                                                2011034285

13-digit ISBN: 978-1-57922-643-5 (cloth)
13-digit ISBN: 978-1-57922-644-2 (paper)
13-digit ISBN: 978-1-57922-645-9 (library networkable e-edition)
13-digit ISBN: 978-1-57922-646-6 (consumer e-edition)

Printed in the United States of America

All first editions printed on acid-free paper
that meets the American National Standards Institute
Z39-48 Standard.

Bulk Purchases

Quantity discounts are available for use in workshops
and for staff development.
Call 1-800-232-0223

Second Edition, 2012

*To all the new PhDs and about-to-be PhDs
who will read this book*

*In memory of my mother,
Belle Epstein Drew
1919–2002
To my grandchildren,
Megan and Daniel
and
To their parents,
Kristin and Rusty*

—David Drew

To my wife, Muriel

—Paul Gray

ACKNOWLEDGMENTS

The authors and Stylus Publishing, LLC, acknowledge *Inside Higher Ed*, *The Chronicle of Higher Education*, Rick Reis's electronic newsletter *Tomorrow's Professor*,[1] and a number of doctoral seminars for providing forums for presenting a number of these hints. We are particularly indebted to Steven Gump, Laura Kazan, Robert E. Machol, and Jack Schuster for their insightful comments and help. Articles in *Inside Higher Ed* by Rob Weir, Eliza Wolf, Thomas Wright, and others inspired several of the new hints in this second edition.

[1] Available at http://cgi.stanford.edu/~dept-ctl/cgi-bin/tomprof/postings.php.

CONTENTS

Foreword 1 to the First Edition by Laurie Richlin   xxi

Foreword 2 to the First Edition by Steadman Upham   xxv

Introduction   1

CHAPTER ONE: BASIC CONCEPTS

1   Gray's theorem of $N + 2$ 9
2   Most academic fields are dominated by fewer than 100
    powerful people   9
3   How to become known   9
4   Drew's law on publishing papers   10
5   Make sure you have a mentor   10
6   Specialize—Get known for something   10

CHAPTER TWO: THE PhD

7   Finish your PhD as early as possible   13
8   Be humble about your PhD   13
9   A PhD is primarily an indication of survivorship   13
10   A PhD is a certification of research ability based on a
     sample of 1   14
11   A PhD is a license to reproduce   14

12 You must have the PhD in hand before you can move up
    the academic ladder   14
13 The key danger point occurs when you leave highly
    structured coursework   15
14 The PhD and part-time study   15
15 Avoid Watson's syndrome   16
16 Celebrate your PhD   16

CHAPTER THREE: THE DISSERTATION

17 Prelims   21
18 Finding a dissertation topic   22
19 Problem-solving mode   23
20 Put a lot of effort into writing your dissertation proposal 23
21 The range of your literature review   23
22 Selecting the dissertation advisory committee   24
23 The dissertation abstract   24
24 How long is too long for your dissertation?   24
25 The chain of references   25
26 Match the literature search to the discussion of results
    and the conclusions   25
27 The risk of nonsignificant results   25
28 The dissertation defense   26

CHAPTER FOUR: JOB HUNTING

29 Job hunting is a research project   31
30 Pick a place where you and your family want to live   31
31 When to apply for a faculty position   31
32 Find the best possible school for your first job   32
33 Change your academic field or move every seven years   32
34 Not-for-profit or for-profit for your first or second job? 33
35 Exceptions to the previous hint   34
36 Build a reference pool   34

37	Résumés are important	35
38	Dual careers	35
39	The short list	35

Job Opportunities 36

40	The law of supply and demand	37
41	Research- versus teaching-oriented institutions	38
42	The jobs may be at for-profit institutions	38
43	New programs	39
44	National rankings	39
45	Teaching in a community college	40
46	Online universities	41
47	The assistant dean strategy	41
48	Evaluate a postdoc carefully	42
49	Nonacademic opportunities	43
50	Nonuniversity research organizations	43
51	Teaching overseas for fun and profit	44

Interviewing 45

52	Tactics for interviewing	45
53	Dressing for the job interview	46
54	Don't be intimidated by the schools your interviewers attended	46
55	Interview your potential bosses	47
56	Dealing with interviewers who have published less than you have	47
57	Prepare an elevator speech	47

Data Gathering 48

58	Determine the cultures	48
59	Gather salary and tenure data	49
60	Obtaining information on tenure levels is a little trickier	49
61	Ask about the retirement system	49

62 Parking   50
63 Determine real pay   51

Offers   51
64 Get the offer in writing, read it, and negotiate before you
      accept   51
65 Get your PhD before you start the tenure track, unless
      you are starving or homeless   52
66 Avoid taking your first job at a school you attended   53
67 Choosing among offers   53

Hunting for the Next Job   54
68 Positioning yourself for the next job   54
69 If you become unemployed   55

CHAPTER FIVE: TEACHING

70 Publications are the only form of portable wealth   61
71 Many colleges and universities value teaching   61
72 Teaching is a learned art   61
73 Being a mentor   62
74 Go to Toastmasters International   62
75 Meeting classes is paramount   63
76 Teaching can be a dangerous profession   63
77 Consider costs to students when selecting textbooks   64
78 Don't let committee work erode your commitment to
      teaching and mentoring   64

In the Classroom   64
79 Summaries lock in the material   64
80 Encourage questions   65
81 Enjoy your classes   65
82 Lecturing versus facilitating   65
83 Teaching is not synonymous with lecturing   66

84   Lecture capture   66
85   Obtaining student responses through technology
         (clickers)   67
86   PowerPoint presentations   68

Teaching Online   68
87   Distance education   68
88   Distance learning is a blessing and a threat   69

Students   70
89   Be wary of student excuses   70
90   Believe it or not, cheating is widespread   70
91   Teach every student   70
92   Teach to the student's frame of reference   71
93   Distracted students   71
94   Undergraduates don't recall much from seven or more
         years ago   72
95   Will this be on the final?   72
96   Grade inflation   73
97   Keep up with technobabble   74
98   Wikipedia and other Web sources   74
99   Letters of reference for students   75
100   The student as customer mantra   75

CHAPTER SIX: RESEARCH
101   If you want a research career, make sure the position you
         are offered allows you to actually do research   81
102   You can trade off teaching loads and research
         opportunities   82
103   Research requires quantitative and qualitative skills   82
104   Learn grantsmanship   82
105   Don't be modest when writing a grant proposal   83
106   Protest if your brilliant grant proposal is declined   83

107   Build an advisory panel of nationally respected experts
      into your grant proposal   83
108   If you didn't build in an advisory panel, it's not too late   84
109   Get the grant approval in writing   84
110   Get clearance before you study an organization   84
111   Institutional review boards (IRBs)   85
112   Academic trade journals are sources of higher education
      (and job) information   86
113   Collaborate and cooperate   86
114   Plagiarism is a no-no   87
115   Back up, back up, back up your research   87
116   Of the people who receive a PhD, the mode for the
      number of publications is 0 followed closely by 1   88

CHAPTER SEVEN: TENURE

117   Tenure is the prize   91
118   Your promotion dossier   91
119   Why tenure is such a hurdle   92
120   If by chance you achieve tenure, never take another
      appointment without it   93
121   Tenure, like research support, can be negotiated on the
      way in   93
122   Tenure is tougher to obtain in cross-disciplinary fields   93
123   Tenure is forever (almost)   94
124   Tenure as we know it today may not be here forever   94
125   The number of tenured slots may decrease with time   95

The Mechanics of Tenure   95
126   The tenure clock is really four and a half years, not seven   95
127   The Dreaded Impact Factor   95
128   Tenure committees look almost exclusively at refereed
      publications   96

129	Download counts	96
130	Multiple-author papers	97
131	Publication quality counts	97
132	Rolling reviews	98

CHAPTER EIGHT: ACADEMIC RANK

133	Being a tenured full professor is as close to freedom as you can come	103
134	As a full professor, you must be known for something	103
135	Avoid becoming the pitied Permanent Associate Professor	104
136	Promotion is a unique opportunity for a larger pay raise	104

CHAPTER NINE: YOUR FINANCIAL LIFE AS AN ACADEMIC

137	Academics are risk averse	107
138	Contracts are given to faculty for nine months	107
139	Salaries vary by field	107
140	Summer pay	108
141	The zero raise years	108
142	Retirement savings	108
143	Tax deferral	110
144	Administrators make more	111

CHAPTER TEN: LIFE AS AN ACADEMIC

145	Good deans/bad deans	115
146	Never, ever choose sides in department politics	115
147	Don't accept a joint appointment	115
148	Join the faculty club	115
149	Office hours	116
150	Sabbaticals	116
151	Maintain collegiality	117

152	As an academic, you are a public person	117
153	Freedom of speech	118
154	Attend invited lectures	118
155	Serving as an external reviewer	119
156	Keeping up with your field	121
157	You can go home again—retreat rights	121
158	The board of trustees	121

Your Administrative Life 122

159	Secretaries/administrative assistants are a scarce resource	123
160	Value your teaching assistants and graders	123
161	Grading	123
162	Your research assistants require supervision	123
163	Physical plant	124
164	Be careful what you delegate	124
165	Business cards	125

Your Digital Life 125

166	Learn the idiosyncrasies of your institution's computer center	126
167	Be realistic about what your computer can do for you	126
168	The downside of e-mail	127
169	Don't get on too many e-mail lists	128
170	Your students love e-mail, texting, and Twitter	128
171	Keep up with computer developments	128
172	Meetings and digital publications	130
173	Interlibrary loans are quicker and more efficient than they used to be	130
174	Use digital collections if they are available in your field	130
175	Telecommuting	131
176	Your website	131
177	Your Web visibility	132
178	The persistence of language	133

Institutional Citizen 133

179 Get to know the development people in your school and support them 133

180 Be responsive to the alumni office 134

181 When you do something noteworthy, let your school's public relations department know 134

182 Communicating your field to the public 134

183 The Faculty Senate in most institutions provides a forum 135

184 Service 135

Department Chair 136

185 Never, ever become a department chair (even an acting department chair) unless you're a tenured full professor 136

186 Be aware that the powers of a department chair are few 137

187 The role conflict in the job 138

188 Leadership 138

189 Dealing with student problems 138

190 The redeeming social values of being chair 139

191 Don't stay in the chair position too long 139

Travel and Conferences 139

192 Professional travel 139

193 Attend conferences 140

194 Choosing your conferences 141

195 Abstracts help you get on conference programs 141

196 Your conference presentation 142

197 Protect your intellectual capital while traveling 142

198 Drew's rule of conference redundancy 143

Grievances 143

199 You may become involved in a student grievance 143

200 Sexual harassment 144

201 Faculty rarely volunteer to serve on the grievance
     committee   144
202 You may become the grievant against your institution   144

Dealing With Myths   145
203 Myth 1: Faculty enjoy lots of free time   145
204 Myth 2: Faculty's political leanings   145

CHAPTER ELEVEN: DIVERSITY
205 The continuing goal   150
206 Variations among institutions   151
207 Assessing colleagues and deans   151
208 Indicators of true diverse hiring   151
209 The climate for women in academia   152
210 Disabilities   152
211 Workload for underrepresented faculty   152

CHAPTER TWELVE: ON WRITING
212 Learn how to write clearly   157
213 Learn the fine points of English   157
214 Be sure to spell-check, grammar-check, and fact-check
     your work   158
215 Editing your own material   158
216 Limits on self-plagiarism   158
217 Citations   159
218 Develop a pool of research references stored in your
     computer   159
219 Reuse the literature search from your dissertation   160
220 Deadlines are friends, not enemies   160

CHAPTER THIRTEEN: ON PUBLISHING
221 Submit your papers to the best journals in the field   165
222 Write most of your papers for refereed journals   165

223 Avoid writing introductory textbooks 165
224 Recognize the difference between writing the first paper
    on a subject and writing the nth one 166
225 Writing the nth paper means . . . 166
226 When writing the nth paper, make your contribution to
    the issue clear 167
227 Revise papers quickly 167
228 Turn your reviews of other people's papers around quickly 167
229 Publish "early and often," as they say in Chicago politics 167
230 Your dissertation is a publishing asset 168
231 The literature search you performed for your dissertation
    is a treasure trove 168
232 Include single-author papers in your portfolio 168
233 Coauthoring a paper with a superstar 169
234 Be aware of the delays in publishing 169
235 Rewards for academic publishing 170

Journals 171
236 Don't become an editor too early 173
237 Do serve as a reviewer 173

Book Publishers 173
238 Pay attention to the book publishers' representatives who
    come to your office 173
239 Selecting a publisher involves trade-offs 174
240 Get to know the major editors 175

CHAPTER FOURTEEN: PERSONAL CONSIDERATIONS
241 Learn new things over time 179
242 Sequential careers 179
243 Being an expert witness 180
244 Whistle-blowing 181
245 Don't be a penny-ante thief 182

246 Learn time management 182
247 The meaning of your work will change over time 183
248 Completion time 183
249 Failure is an opportunity 184

CHAPTER FIFTEEN: FINAL THOUGHTS
250 "The rich get richer" 187
251 Treat students as though they were guests in your home 187

CHAPTER SIXTEEN: CONCLUSION AND ENVOI

Envoi 191

APPENDICES
APPENDIX A: MECHANICS OF THE DISSERTATION
252 Oral examinations 195
253 Visual aids in oral presentations 196
254 Waiting for the committee's decision after the oral
examination 197
255 Post–oral exam rewrites 197
256 Faculty signatures 198
257 External examiners 199
258 Guests at your dissertation defense 199
259 Handing in the dissertation to the registrar 200

APPENDIX B: OUTSIDE INCOME
260 Consulting as a hired hand 201
261 Don't live on your consulting income 202
262 Consulting income is taxable 202
263 Grants and contracts 202

264 The summer teaching option   203
265 Hire a tax specialist to fill out form 1040   203
266 Pro bono work   204
267 Consulting pay rate   204
268 Warning! You can't teach elsewhere for outside money   205

APPENDIX C:
HOW TO BECOME A MILLIONAIRE

269 Making (or not making) a fortune through publishing
       and public appearances   206
270 Write a best-selling novel   208
271 You may want to use a pseudonym for nonacademic
       publications   208
272 Start your own consulting firm   209
273 Write a college textbook   209
274 Write a textbook for K–12 education   210
275 Write a crossover book   210
276 Save in a TIAA–CREF or other annuity plan   211

APPENDIX D: WRITING HINTS

277 Explain only what the reader needs to know   212
278 Avoid passive voice   212
279 Avoid *should* and *must*   213
280 Avoid using too much boldface and italics   213
281 You can rarely be both *effective* and *efficient*   213
282 Avoid generalizing from a single case   213
283 Don't be afraid to use numbered or bulleted lists   213
284 Use figures and tables   214
285 Learn to use styles in word processing programs   214
286 Use the spell-checker   214
287 Pay special attention to references   215

288   Eliminate poor writing habits   216
289   Bad words   216

APPENDIX E: YOUR HEALTH

290   Avoid stress   219
291   Start a health and fitness program   220
292   Exercise   221
293   Addictions   221
294   Weight control   222
295   Diet   222
296   Meditation   223
297   Acupuncture   223
298   Physical appearance   224
299   Health and life insurance   225

About the Authors   227

FOREWORD 1 TO THE FIRST EDITION

What I Wished I Had Known

FOR 20 YEARS I HAVE WORKED with faculty members at all types of institutions, from small colleges through large universities, on how to design their courses to facilitate, assess, and document learning. During that time I also have taught hundreds of graduate students interested in an academic career. Although professors are deeply concerned about their subjects, their students' learning, and their institutions' culture, most receive no preparation to deal with the complex issues involved in being a faculty member. This lack of understanding is doubly true for graduate students preparing for academic careers. Of course, neither group should be expected to know how to become or be a faculty member: In almost all cases no one ever taught them how to improve learning or participate in campus governance. Just as teachers do not expect students to learn how to perform complex tasks without study, practice, and feedback, faculty members cannot be effective academic citizens or instructors without similar processes.

All hint numbers and titles in this foreword have been modified to reflect the new edition. Foreword authors' titles and institutional affiliations have been updated.—Ed.

I long ago realized what a particularly lucky person I was to receive my committee's guidance to complete my doctoral program and move into a university career. Since then, as I have researched graduate student advising and mentoring, I have found that across graduate programs and institutions, students report uncertainty about deciding on dissertation topics, finding an academic job, and what will be required of them to be a success as a professor. What distinguishes this book is that it provides, in one place, the guidance and the help that graduate students and faculty members need to achieve their professional goals.

What I find useful about this book is that Gray and Drew approach faculty work as a job as well as a career. The ideas apply equally to experienced, veteran faculty members and to the graduate students I teach in my university's Preparing Future Faculty Program. They make it clear that being a scholar means more than loving your subject. Through their wry "hints," they guide the reader a behind-the-scenes look to

- GRADUATE SCHOOL: a short time in the course of an academic career (we hope), but a busy one for survivorship (Hint 9: *A PhD is primarily an indication of survivorship*); finding mentors (2: *Most academic fields are dominated by fewer than 100 powerful people*); getting known (6: *Specialize—Get known for something*); and, most of all, finishing (13: *The key danger point occurs when you leave highly structured coursework*).
- JOB HUNTING: a research process that begins almost the first day of graduate school, and involves everything from a lifestyle choice (30: *Pick a place where you and your family want to live*) to understanding disciplinary "supply and demand."
- PUBLISHING: most importantly Drew's law that every study can be published somewhere (Hint 4) and Gray's theorem that tenure requires $N + 2$ publications where $N =$ the number you have (Hint 1). Publishing also requires learning how to

write (214: *Be sure to spell-check, grammar-check, and fact-check your work*), and how to negotiate the publishing world (221: *Submit your best papers to the best journals in the field;* 227: *Revise papers quickly;* 229: *Publish "early and often," as they say in Chicago politics*) and other editorial and writing hints.

- TEACHING AND SERVICE: being a good teacher (70: "Teaching is a great personal satisfaction and is an important public good that you perform") and academic citizen (146: *Never, ever choose sides in department politics;* 148: *Join the faculty club;* 179: *Get to know the development people in your school and support them*) may not be what many graduate students think about when choosing the professorial career, but as the authors point out, both make a big impact on success at an institution.

- ADMINISTRATION: Gray and Drew deal forthrightly with administration (144: *Administrators make more*), the challenges of the usual first step, becoming a department chair (185: *Never, never become a department chair [even an acting department chair] unless you are a tenured full professor;* 191: *Don't stay in the chair position too long*), and the possibility of joint administration and teaching appointments leading to the tenure track (47: *The assistant dean strategy*).

- TENURE AND PROMOTION: this is the goal toward which the new academics point their work. The special sections on tenure and academic rank, in particular, provide the straightforward set of recommendations no one else will tell you. Tenure (109: *Get the grant approval in writing;* 126: *The tenure clock is really four and a half years, not seven;* 120: *If by chance you achieve tenure, never take another appointment without it*) and Academic Rank (133: *Being a tenured full professor is as close to freedom as you can come;* 135: *Avoid becoming the pitied Permanent Associate Professor*).

Gray and Drew include appendices on the mechanics of the dissertation, outside income, writing hints, and—very importantly—health considerations for facing the rigors of an academic job.

This book is full of wonderful, witty, and, of course, true suggestions from two experienced mentors about the academic career.

Finally, I propose an additional hint for those who wish to become superb professors:

300: *Read this book.*

Laurie Richlin
Director, Office of Faculty Development
Charles R. Drew University of Medicine and Science
Los Angeles, California

FOREWORD 2 TO THE
FIRST EDITION

I WILL NEVER FORGET MY FIRST DAY OF graduate school at Arizona State University in 1976. I entered the west door of the Anthropology Building after parking in the small lot that I later learned was reserved for the department's full professors. Down a half flight of stairs and there I was, thrust into a series of winding hallways and closed doors that held faculty offices, archaeology labs, storage rooms, graduate assistant cubicles, and the office of the archaeology laboratory supervisor (and the most important person for me during that first year), Mrs. Laughlin.

My journey toward the PhD had begun, and my profoundest memories of those first few months center not on the subjects I was studying, but on the closed and locked doors in the anthropology building. I knew that behind each door was a professor I did not know, a new body of knowledge I wanted to learn, new graduate student colleagues I wished to meet, exotic collections of artifacts I would eventually study, and various tools of the trade with which I was unfamiliar (laser transits, magnetometers, and the peculiar aluminum cubes used to take samples for archaeomagnetic dating).

All hint numbers and titles in this foreword have been modified to reflect the new edition. Foreword authors' titles and institutional affiliations have been updated.—Ed.

Slowly, over the course of four and a half years, I would gain access to each of those doors in the anthropology building, and to the treasures, challenges, and curiosities that formed my path to both a master's degree and PhD in anthropology and archaeology.

Mrs. Laughlin was my first guide to graduate school during those formative months. She informed me of lab protocols, advised me about the personality quirks of various professors, steered me to key resources in the library and special collections, and was a kind of confidante after class grades were given and feelings were bruised. But most importantly, Mrs. Laughlin held the keys to all of the locked doors in the archaeology wing of the building, and it was through Mrs. Laughlin that I began to gain access to the spaces and tools of archaeology at ASU.

What They Didn't Teach You in Graduate School provides the same kind of crucial information for graduate students that I gleaned from Mrs. Laughlin. There is an unwritten code of conduct for graduate students, and there are many rules of the road that can only be learned from someone who has taken the journey. Professors Gray and Drew do a remarkable job of delivering both the code and the rules, and they do so with wit, insight, humor, and the voice of experience. This is not surprising, since Paul Gray and David Drew are consummate academics—award-winning teachers, world-class researchers, and the kind of colleagues that make for valued and lifelong friends.

More importantly, Gray and Drew go well beyond the graduate student years to offer counsel and advice to beginning faculty members about the mysteries of university life. Their hints and aphorisms provide a priceless guide to the sometimes odd, unpredictable, and counterintuitive culture of academe. Gray and Drew explain the intricacies of faculty life, discuss the all-important quality of collegiality, and reflect on great teaching and the conduct of significant research. Several of the issues they highlight are worth noting.

First is mentoring. One simply cannot overestimate the importance of a mentor. Often, we tend to think of mentoring as something that is done to us while we are graduate students. But Gray and Drew point out how mentors are important for each of us at every stage of our career. And as one receives mentoring, even as a faculty member, it is vital for faculty to keep the chain of support intact by mentoring graduate students and junior colleagues in the department.

Second are indisposition and procrastination. Many pitfalls dot the path to a higher degree, or to tenure and promotion. Watson's syndrome (Hint 15) has derailed more graduate students and wrecked more academic careers than any other single cause I can think of. I have seen it time and time again during the 30-plus years I have spent in academe. Never-ending literature reviews and eternal computer runs to crunch the last bit of life out of a data set are excuses for not drawing conclusions or taking a position on an important issue. As Gray and Drew point out, such frailties will be quickly noted by more experienced academics, and presage an early exit from academe.

Third is computers. Digital resources are not just important to your academic career, they are absolutely vital (see Hints 166 through 178). Digital tools enhance productivity and are the currency of communication with today's students. You can choose to be a Luddite, but if you do you will be standing in the unemployment line still wondering if the best fountain pens are made by Delta or Waterman.

Finally, and of greatest importance to me, is the fundamental message of this book: Value erudition and celebrate enlightened understanding! Gray and Drew make it clear that they "consider *professor* to be the best job available on the planet" and universities to be "wonderful, and occasionally transcendent, places to work." I heartily agree with this assessment. These qualities flow from a community of scholars that is organized around the love and pursuit of knowledge. *What They Didn't Teach You in Graduate School* is a guide to this astonishing world, and a most useful and entertaining primer on how to be successful and happy in academe. I only wish I had had a copy of this book on my first day of graduate school so many years ago.

Steadman Upham
President, The University of Tulsa
Tulsa, Oklahoma

INTRODUCTION

GRADUATE SCHOOL IS A WONDERFUL, heady time for students, particularly those working toward the highest achievement, the PhD. It is a time when long-term friendships are formed, and a time when the discussion in seminars, classes, and with other graduate students focuses on intellectual life. Yes, there are financial worries, given the expenses and the low pay. Yes, there are the problems of maturing for students fresh out of undergraduate school, and the problems of reentering academia after a long time away for students over 30. Nonetheless, it is a marvelous time in your life, and one that you, like today's professors, will look back on fondly.

When you receive the degree and find your first job, you will be exposed to the realities of academic life. What will it be like? How should you navigate this particular real world you are thrust into? Most students, even those who taught part-time before their degree, have only the vaguest concept of that world. It is the purpose of this book to reduce the uncertainty, to present an irreverent guide to what it is *really* like, at least as seen by the two authors who each spent a long time immersed in this world as well as in the world outside academia.

We deliberately kept this book short, by presenting it in its first edition in the form of 199 hints about what no one told you in graduate school but what you really need to know. In the several years since then we developed an additional 100 hints that are scattered through this second edition. The new material broadly expands the chapters that deal with job hunting, teaching, and our readers' lives as academics. We also strengthened the chapters on research and tenure. We moved most of the material about the dissertation from Appendix A into Chapter 3 and created a new Appendix A on the mechanics of the dissertation process. Under teaching we added major sections on life in the classroom and on dealing with students. We added a section on travel under life as an academic, as professors travel a lot, and a tongue-in-cheek Appendix C on how to become a millionaire while an academic. We made only minor changes on some chapters and appendices, such as Appendix E on health.

Throughout the book we present data that apply to the median of the book's anticipated readership. Because we fully realize the median is representative rather than universal, we qualify many statements with words such as *usually*, because you, the reader, may differ extensively from the median.

Some of the hints are short, others longer. Some of the individual hints are worthy of chapters or books of their own, whereas others are important tidbits to tuck into your head for future reference. We've tried to write the hints with a bit of humor here and there. Don't be put off by that. What we say is indeed true.

Since we suspect you will keep this book and keep referring to it as you face new situations, we've organized the hints into 16 short chapters and 5 appendices. We've added a numerical list of the hints at the beginning so you can find hints when you need them.

This book is written in terms of our experience in the United States. That is the universe we know. We recognize that procedures, rules, and assumptions differ by country, even those as close as Canada and Mexico. If you are outside the United States and are reading this book, please pardon our parochialism.

Our hints are based on what we see today in the world around us. They do not reflect the way we think academia should be or could be. Unfortunately, or fortunately, depending on your point of view, academia moves slowly. Therefore, much of what is in this book will stand you in good stead for a considerable fraction of your career. Changes are in the wind that may affect you. For example, many argue that tenure will not be here forever. Yet, in the short term you will need to deal with it, and we included a chapter about it.

A particular reality of academia is that in a number of fields, jobs for fresh PhDs are scarce. Although you don't like to think about it in pure business terms, the market for PhDs depends on supply and demand and is notoriously difficult to model and predict. Students make decisions about the field they want to enter years before they complete their degrees. Hence you play a futures game in a changing environment. We do know, however, to use that tired cliché: what goes out of fashion comes back into fashion.

Both of us come from a research institution that highly values teaching, as do we. We observe that those with strong research productivity are hired for the most-prized and best-paid positions in higher education. We also observe that many new PhDs see teaching as their highest calling and want to spend their life doing it. Fortunately, the largest employers of faculty are the four-year and community colleges that value teaching first.

In this book we talk not only about the mechanics of being a professor but also the nature of life as an academic. The next six paragraphs present our view of that life.

At colleges or universities, life is divided arbitrarily into semesters or quarters. For convenience, we talk in terms of semesters. Even at the smallest of schools, at the beginning of each semester you (and your students) face new students whom you've never seen before and many of whom you will never see again in class. Classes meet on a heartbeat schedule—for example, Monday, Wednesday, and Friday for one hour—for a fixed number of weeks. Then it is all over, and you start again. After the spring semester, if you don't teach summer school, you are free to do what you want. For most academics, summer becomes a time to prepare for the next academic year and to do research and, perhaps, take some vacation. But summer is soon over, and you start again.

Whereas students change from semester to semester, your faculty colleagues change only slowly. Yes, some people move on or retire, and new people are brought in to take their place (just as you were), but tomorrow's faculty is like today's faculty, only slightly different. They are people you must live with and who must live with you over considerable periods of time. Then there's the administration and the staff, who, like your colleagues, also change only slowly.

With few exceptions, when you take your first job you are off to a new school, often distant from where you formed strong friendships and learned your profession. Like many PhDs starting out, you may find you are the only one in your department who is deep into your specialty in your field. After all, it was your specialty you were hired for.

You will spend a considerable part of your first year just learning about the school and its norms, establishing a social network of people you trust and are compatible with, and preparing the courses you are assigned to teach. If in a research-intensive school, you will also be expected to advance your research; if in a teaching institution, your teaching load will be heavier, and you will serve on more committees. You will also learn about the quality of the students you teach.

It is a good life, and you even get paid.

Many universities offer preparing future faculty (PFF) programs for PhD students. Although the name may differ from school to school, the objective of these programs is essentially the same as this book: to tell PhD students about the world they will soon enter. If your university offers such a program, enroll. You will learn much that is vital for success as a professor. We are such fans of our university's PFF program we asked its founding director, Laurie Richlin, to write one of the forewords for this book.

We've enjoyed writing these hints and hope you will find them useful. We look forward to receiving feedback from you, favorable and unfavorable, confirming or disagreeing with our advice. We hope you will send us new hints, including anything we left out, so we can include them in future editions for future PhDs. We will, of course, credit you for your input.

Paul Gray (paul.gray@cgu.edu)
David E. Drew (david.drew@cgu.edu)
Claremont, California
November 2011

1

BASIC CONCEPTS

HINT 1: GRAY'S THEOREM OF $N + 2$. The number of papers required for tenure is $N + 2$, where N is the number you published.

EACH YEAR PHD CANDIDATES AND young faculty members come into our offices and sheepishly ask us to tell them what they really need to know about building a career in academia. We usually take them to a long lunch and give them the helpful hints we share with you in this book.

1. GRAY'S THEOREM OF $N + 2$. The number of papers required for tenure is $N + 2$, where N is the number you published.

Corollary: Gray's theorem is independent of N.

2. MOST ACADEMIC FIELDS ARE DOMINATED BY FEWER THAN 100 POWERFUL PEOPLE. These people know one another and determine the course of the field. Early in your career you should get to know as many of them as possible. More to the point, they should know who you are. You want them to see you as a bright young person at the forefront of your field. Although this tactic is important, be aware of the dangers associated with it. You should not begin the process until after you've mastered the literature (particularly the papers they wrote!) and developed some ideas of your own. If they get to know you and conclude you have no ideas, you're finished.

3. HOW TO BECOME KNOWN. Think of whom you know in the field:

- People who write books
- People who publish papers in journals
- People who are active in their professional societies

Use this list as a guide for deciding what you can do to become one of the known people.

4. DREW'S LAW ON PUBLISHING PAPERS. Every paper can be published somewhere. Your first papers will be rejected. Don't worry about this. View the reviewer's complete misunderstanding of your brilliance as cheap editorial help. Use his or her advice to revise. Every paper has a market. If *Journal A* rejects it, make the appropriate changes and send it to *Journal B*. If the work is sound, someone will publish it.

5. MAKE SURE YOU HAVE A MENTOR early in your career. The old apprentice system still exists. Try to find mentors who were successful with others, who will support you, and who believe that furthering your career helps their own careers. Such a mentor is preferable to the internationally famous Nobel Prize winner who exploits you.

6. SPECIALIZE—GET KNOWN FOR SOMETHING. It helps visibility. Sadly, brilliant, restless people who work on several topics simultaneously usually do not achieve as much visibility as those who plod along in the same area for many years.

2

THE PhD

HINT 15: AVOID WATSON'S SYNDROME, a euphemism for procrastination.

I T CAN BE ARGUED THAT YOU DO JOB HUNTING (the subject of Chapter 4) before you receive the PhD. However, the PhD is the prize you seek above all from your graduate experience. We therefore discuss it first.

7. FINISH YOUR PHD AS EARLY AS POSSIBLE. Don't feel you need to create the greatest work that Western civilization ever saw. Five years from now the only thing that will matter is whether you finished. If you don't finish, you are likely to join the ranks of freeway flyers, holding multiple part-time teaching jobs.

8. BE HUMBLE ABOUT YOUR PHD. You don't need to flaunt the degree. Everyone has one. Many of your colleagues in your institution and outside it will be put off if you sign everything *Dr.* or *Jane Jones, PhD.* The only time it is appropriate to disregard this Hint is when making reservations at a restaurant. When you call and ask for a table for four for Dr. Jones, you will get more respect and often better seating. In fact, that is the main use for the title of *doctor.*

9. A PHD IS PRIMARILY AN INDICATION OF SURVIVORSHIP. Although the public at large may view your doctorate as a superb intellectual achievement and a reflection of brilliance, you probably know deep in your heart that it is not. It represents a lot of hard work on your part over a long period of time. You probably received help from at least one faculty member to get over rough spots. Your family, be it parents or spouse, stayed with you through the vicissitudes of creating the dissertation. You stuck with it until it was done—

unlike ABDs (all-but-dissertations), who completed all their other requirements but bailed out before they finished their dissertations.

10. A PhD IS A CERTIFICATION OF RESEARCH ABILITY BASED ON A SAMPLE OF 1. The PhD certifies that you are able to do quality research. Unlike the MD, which requires extensive work with patients followed by years of internship and residency, the PhD is based on a single sample: your dissertation. The people who sign your dissertation are making a large bet on your ability to do quality research again and again in the future.

11. A PhD IS A LICENSE TO REPRODUCE and an obligation to maintain the quality of your intellectual descendants. Once you are a PhD, it is possible for you (assuming you are working in an academic department that offers a PhD program) to create new PhDs. Even if your department does not offer a PhD, you can be called upon to sit on PhD examining committees in your own or in neighboring institutions. Yours is a serious responsibility because you are creating your intellectual descendants. Remember that if you vote to pass someone who is marginal or worse, that PhD in turn is given the same privilege. If candidates are not up to standard, it is likely that some of their descendants will not be also. Unlike human intergeneration time which is about 20 years, academics' intergeneration time is 5 years or less. Furthermore, a single individual may supervise 50 or more PhDs over a 30-year career.

12. YOU MUST HAVE THE PhD IN HAND BEFORE YOU CAN MOVE UP THE ACADEMIC LADDER. The world is full of ABDs. We talked about them briefly in Hint 9 and will again in Hint 18. ABDs may be much abler and more brilliant than you but they didn't possess the stamina (or the circumstances) to finish the degree. In our judgment, being an ABD is the end of the academic line.

13. THE KEY DANGER POINT OCCURS WHEN YOU LEAVE HIGHLY STRUCTURED COURSEWORK (Phase 1) and enter the unstructured world of the qualification examination (Hint 17) and the dissertation (Phase 2). Here are two strategies to help you navigate Phase 2.

- Stay in touch with your professors, especially your adviser. One of us insists that students come in for a meeting each week, even if nothing happened. Just the fear of not being able to report anything stimulates the mind.
- Meet regularly, ideally every week, for lunch or dinner or afternoon coffee, with two or three fellow graduate students who are also struggling with Phase 2. Compare notes and progress.

14. THE PhD AND PART-TIME STUDY. Although all PhD students used to be on the campus and often worked as teaching or research assistants part-time, in many fields that attract midcareer students today (for example, education) the norm is to work at an off-campus job full-time and on the PhD part-time. Others, such as computer science students, develop an idea for a start-up company (e.g., the cofounders of Google) and drift from full-time to part-time. We applaud part-time PhD students.

If you are working on your PhD part-time, you will find it difficult enough in Phase 1 to tell your boss that you can't attend that nighttime budget crisis meeting or tell your spouse that you can't go to your child's soccer game because you must be in class. It is even more difficult when you're in Phase 2 to tell him or her that you won't be there because you must be home, in your study, staring at a blank computer screen trying to get past writer's block.

As a part-time student, you need to find ways (in addition to the suggested strategies in Hint 13) to be physically present on campus. You can do so in many ways, such as spending time writing in a library carrel.[1] Physical presence is important psychologically. If you never visit campus and become caught up in your work and family activities, you face the danger that your uncompleted PhD program can begin to seem like something you used to do in a faraway time and place.

15. AVOID WATSON'S SYNDROME. Named by R. J. Gelles, this syndrome is a euphemism for procrastination.[2] It involves doing everything possible to avoid completing work. It differs from writer's block in that the sufferer substitutes real work that distracts from doing what is necessary for completing the dissertation or for advancing toward an academic career. The work may be outside or inside the university. Examples given by Gelles include

- home remodeling
- a never-ending literature review (after all, new papers are being published all the time and they must be referenced)
- data paralysis—making seemingly infinite Statistical Analysis System (SAS) and Statistical Package for the Social Sciences (SPSS) runs
- perfectionism that doesn't let you submit until you think it is perfect (and it never is perfect)

If you suffer from Watson's syndrome, finding a mentor (see Hint 5) who pushes you to finish will help you get it done. For many, however, particularly those who always waited until the night before an examination to begin studying, the syndrome is professionally fatal.

16. CELEBRATE YOUR PhD. When you hand in your signed dissertation and pay the last fee the university exacts from you, go out and Celebrate! Celebrate! Celebrate! You've achieved something marvelous, and you are one of a very small number in the population who can say you are a PhD. A rough calculation shows that about 3 out of 400 adults in the United States hold a PhD. Attaining a PhD is a big deal. Honor that.

Celebrations are also called for when you pass your qualifying examination, when your dissertation proposal is accepted, and when you successfully defend your dissertation. Be sure to attend your graduation ceremony so you can share your achievement with your family.

A PhD, like life, is a journey. It marks the end of one stage and the beginning of what lies ahead. Don't fail to appreciate the moment of your accomplishment. Yes, other big moments await you. But like almost every PhD, you've never had a moment this big, and it will be a long time before you have another one that matches it.

Notes

1. The library is a large building filled with books and journals. It functions sort of like Google, but on a deeper level.

2. This hint is based on R. J. Gelles, "Watson's Syndrome," *Inside Higher Ed*, June 19, 2006, http://www.insidehighered.com/workplace/2006/06/19/gelles.

3

THE DISSERTATION

HINT 17: PRELIMS. Rule 1: Find out about
the format well before you take prelims.

W E PUT OUR THOUGHTS ON THE DISSERTATION into this early chapter because for readers who are graduate students, the dissertation is the largest single hurdle they must leap over to achieve the PhD. This chapter is supplemented by Appendix A, which describes the mechanics involved in the end stages of the dissertation process once it has been written and approved by the adviser. The appendix covers the time from the oral defense to handing the dissertation in to the registrar.

If you already have your PhD, you can skip this chapter and Appendix A for now, but they will be of help to you later when you become a member of a PhD advisory committee.

17. PRELIMS. To obtain a PhD almost everyone takes a preliminary, or qualifying, examination, commonly known as *prelims* or *quals.* The purpose of prelims is to demonstrate you understand and can explain your major field and are sufficiently knowledgeable to undertake a dissertation. You must pass prelims before you can advance to candidacy. The number of times you can take prelims is usually limited, although you can petition for another chance. If you fail all attempts, you must leave the graduate program.

The content and format varies by field and by school. In the formal sit-down format you are examined in specified subfields.[1] The exams cover several days, and each part is allocated a fixed time.

Rule 1: Find out about the format well before you take prelims.

Prelims are highly stressful before you take them but most PhD students (at least those who pass) fondly remember them afterward as being "trivial" or an "integrating exercise," among other similarly endearing qualifiers. The stress is real. Few PhD students prepare alone. Students form study groups that meet periodically to compare notes, test one another, prepare sample responses to previous questions, and offer encouragement. Asking students who passed the prelims about their experiences helps reduce your anxiety. Knowing who is preparing each question also reduces uncertainty.

In most cases, when you pass all but one part of the prelims, you can petition to retake that part.

Rule 2: Determine the best time for you to take prelims.

Unless your department or school specifies the timing of your prelims, you have some freedom of choice. If you take them too early (e.g., the semester you arrive) you are likely to fail. If you take them too late or at the last possible moment, you risk increasing the time to degree. If you wait too long, most of the people who arrived the same time as you have already taken them, and your study group will be mostly people you don't know well. Furthermore, since faculty and courses change, prelims test you on different material over time.

18. FINDING A DISSERTATION TOPIC is not as easy as it looks. In fact, for a lot of students it is the most difficult part of their dissertation. (Many students begin erroneously believing that defining a topic is supposed to be the easiest part of the dissertation. "If I'm having so much trouble with the easiest part of this task, how will I ever finish?") Some students go to a professor they want to work with and ask for suggestions for a topic. Usually they wind up desperately unhappy because they don't own the topic but are condemned to work on it. Often these students spend the rest of their lives as ABDs.

19. PROBLEM-SOLVING MODE. Don't assume that if you are having trouble defining a dissertation topic then the entire dissertation process will be that arduous. Once you define the topic, you are in problem-solving mode, and most people do well in solving a problem once they know what the topic is.

20. PUT A LOT OF EFFORT INTO WRITING YOUR DISSERTATION PROPOSAL. The proposal has two important payoffs.

1. It usually provides one or more chapters of your end product, the dissertation.
2. It is a contract between you and your advisory committee on what you must do to receive the degree. In general, if you do well what you promise in the proposal, the committee should sign the final document. If you cannot accomplish all you set out to do, you have the basis for negotiation. For example, if the difference is caused by circumstances (e.g., a data site becomes unavailable) or you developed new results that differ from what you promised, the negotiation is about whether you did enough. Without an agreed-upon proposal, your committee can keep asking for more and more without end.

21. THE RANGE OF YOUR LITERATURE REVIEW. If little or nothing is written on your dissertation topic, don't assume that an abbreviated literature review is acceptable. Dissertation committees are used to a minimum-size review and will insist on it. If only three previous papers even touch on your subject, reviewing just them is not considered an adequate literature search. Furthermore, the new data you expect to obtain, even in a specialized topic, can affect a lot of intersecting fields. Those fields should be identified. In short, a literature review not only discusses what is already done and why, it also points out the areas in which your work has implications.

22. Selecting the dissertation advisory committee. Be skillful in selecting your dissertation advisory committee. The worst possible approach is to pick people because they are famous in their field. Rather, be aware that the role of the advisory committee is to actually help you. Therefore, choose people who can really help you over the rough spots. If your dissertation is experimental and requires expertise in two fields, pick an expert in each field and someone who knows about experimental design and statistics. When push comes to shove (and it will at some time while you are working on your dissertation), the people you need will be there to help you because they made a commitment to you. Simply hoping the expert will contribute time to your problem without being on the committee can prove to be naïve.

23. The dissertation abstract. Once you complete a good presentable dissertation draft, it is time to write your abstract.

Do not underestimate the importance of the abstract—it is more than a bureaucratic afterthought. Many people whom you expect to read the entire dissertation only read the abstract. They include people who might hire you, such as faculty on search committees and deans at institutions you apply to. Furthermore, only the abstract appears, not surprisingly, in dissertation abstracts databases.

Your institution limits abstracts to a maximum number of words. Unfortunately a short abstract is more difficult to write than a long one. Try to summarize your research question, methods, and key findings succinctly and accurately. Also, think of the abstract as a public relations statement. Include references to powerful theories you tested, impressive models you applied or developed, and advanced techniques you employed. Don't be shy.

24. How long is too long for your dissertation? How short is too short? No strict guidelines exist for the length of a dissertation.

Because field and institutional differences exist, we can only provide generic guidelines.

In our experience, the median length for the body of a dissertation is about 125 double-spaced pages. (This figure does not include the abstract, front matter, references or appendices.) We estimate that 80% of the dissertations we have seen ran between 90 and 150 pages of main text. The length tends to be at the short end in the sciences and at the long end in the humanities.

We strongly believe dissertation quality always trumps dissertation length. We are sure your faculty committee members agree.

25. THE CHAIN OF REFERENCES is vital in doing a literature search. Begin with one or two recent articles (a survey article helps), and look at the references that are cited. Then read the publications that seem apropos and look at their reference lists. Repeat this process. Some things will pop up often, and they are usually (but not invariably) the classics in the field that you must include in your references. Proceed from reference to reference until the law of diminishing returns takes over.

26. MATCH THE LITERATURE SEARCH TO THE DISCUSSION OF RE-SULTS AND THE CONCLUSIONS. You may find that as your dissertation progresses, some parts of your literature search are really irrelevant to your research. In this case, you should be ruthless. Despite the brilliance of your prose and the long, tedious hours you put into creating the material, you must delete these pearls. Of course, you should save what you don't use as part of your file of references (Hint 218) so you can use it over and over in future publications.

27. THE RISK OF NONSIGNIFICANT RESULTS. When you select a dissertation topic and write a proposal, be it qualitative or quantitative, you confidently expect to obtain significant results. Significance involves two dimensions:

1. The results are important to the field.
2. The results are statistically significant or produce new insights and understandings.

It is perfectly possible that your results don't show the effect you predicted, or the analysis does not meet standard statistical significance tests, or you were not able to find a second or third data site you promised in your proposal. This risk, although usually small, is there in all dissertations; it's a form of the promise-performance gap.

What do you do if it happens to you? In almost every case, you shouldn't give up or quit your pursuit of the PhD. Follow plan B. Yes, you must convince your adviser (and your committee) that you needn't start over. But you obtained a lot of data during your work, and the data can be used to show, for example, that

- the methodology you used is correct, but the desired effect is not there with this methodology on your particular sample, and
- with a meta-analysis based on adding your results to others, the existing theory is stronger (or weaker) than previously thought.

28. THE DISSERTATION DEFENSE. The dissertation oral defense before an august group of senior faculty is almost always a love feast. Most advisers won't let their students into the examination room if there is even a one-in-a-million chance they will fail. Remember, the adviser's reputation is on the line as well as yours.

When you're finished with your dissertation, you know more about the subject than anyone else in the room. If you suspect that someone on the committee hadn't yet read your dissertation, be kind and explain it in "See Dick. See Jane. See Dick and Jane run up the hill" terms.

If you can't answer a question, say so. Don't fumble and stumble. The inquisitor will ask another one. The following occurred to one of the authors (whom we'll call "I") at his oral defense. At that time, the examination consisted of a defense of the dissertation and any questions examiners chose to ask. A true éminence grise in the field inquired about a topic he was the world's expert on, and I knew little about it. After taking it as far as possible, I said, "That's all I know." The inquisitor then asked if my wife was in the sciences. When I said no, he asked, "How do you explain your field to your wife?" I admired the question as he asked it. I passed.

Note

1. Another format has been used by the very large electrical engineering department at Stanford University, in which students and faculty perform the equivalent of speed dating. Students go from professor's office to professor's office for a 15-minute oral examination on each professor's subject area, with 12 minutes between examinations. It's a brutal format but efficient for the student and the faculty.

4

JOB HUNTING

HINT 58: DETERMINE THE CULTURES . . . find out whether members of the faculty like one another.

THE HINTS IN THIS SECTION ARE directed primarily at those who seek to earn their living in academe. To get in, you must first be offered a job. That first job will strongly affect the rest of your academic life. If you decide you don't want to go into academe or you don't find an academic job, see Hint 49. If you become unemployed, see Hint 69.

29. JOB HUNTING IS A RESEARCH PROJECT, and you should treat it as such. Gather as much information as possible. Read the ads. Contact sources. Follow up leads. Be aggressive. Use your contacts (see Hint 2). The chance of landing a good appointment is higher if you search broadly than if you sit in your office waiting for one or two possibilities. Begin job hunting early, and make it a project you do along with your other work. If you are a graduate student, don't wait until your dissertation is finished to start looking (but see Hint 65).

30. PICK A PLACE WHERE YOU AND YOUR FAMILY WANT TO LIVE that matches your lifestyle. City people are not happy in isolated college towns, and small-town people find it hard to adjust to a megalopolis.

31. WHEN TO APPLY FOR A FACULTY POSITION. For PhD candidates, the timing of your job application will be determined by your progress in completing the degree and your financial situation.

All things being equal, we recommend applying while you are nearing completion of your degree, after your proposal is approved, and you are well along on your dissertation. Don't wait until your dissertation is completed, approved, and turned in. Although you don't want job hunting to interfere with the successful completion of your dissertation, you don't want to graduate and then wonder, "Where will I work next year?"

32. FIND THE BEST POSSIBLE SCHOOL FOR YOUR FIRST JOB. You can only go down in the pecking order, not up, if you don't make it at your first position. If you are a success, you can go up one level at a time. Stanford University doesn't hire from Winsocki Community College.

33. CHANGE YOUR ACADEMIC FIELD OR MOVE EVERY SEVEN YEARS if you really want a broader challenge. This advice seems to run counter to our advice to obtain tenure as soon as possible. It is not. As we say in Hint 121, tenure can be negotiated on the way in.

So why change? It improves your salary. At higher education institutions, people are hired at the national market rate but are given raises based on the internal annual percentage increase. Moving is often the only way to maintain parity or gain a major increase in salary and perquisites.

Change also broadens your outlook. Some broadening is the result of the Hawthorne effect. That is, people pay attention to you because you are new. In the first few years at the new institution or department you will have the aura of the outside expert. After a while, you are just one of the same old crowd.

Changing fields allows you to move from a mature area to a new or more dynamic one. That's where the fun is. It is also an opportunity to get in on the ground floor of a new development. However, you must be careful. Move only to adjacent fields where you can use most of your tools, because changing careers involves some retooling. Radical swings such as moving from French to cognitive psychology or electrical engineering are usually impossible without a second PhD.

34. NOT-FOR-PROFIT OR FOR-PROFIT FOR YOUR FIRST OR SECOND JOB?[1] Most U.S. colleges and universities are not-for-profit, which means they can make a profit but they can't give it to anyone. In particular, they can't give it to stockholders because there aren't any. They rely on the government, endowments, and private donations to make up the difference between tuition income and expenses.

Stockholders or owners of for-profits seek to maximize the return from their investments. A 2010 U.S. Government sampling of for-profits found extensive fraud, particularly in obtaining government support for students.[2] The tragedy for students is that with low graduation rates, high tuition, and high debt, a large fraction of them are doomed to spend a decade or more paying off their debt without a degree to show for it.

There are a lot of for-profit educational institutions. An incomplete list on Wikipedia in 2010 showed 135 for-profit colleges in the United States, many of them chains with multiple locations offering everything from associate degrees to PhDs, from liberal arts to medicine. Perhaps the largest is the University of Phoenix with 225,000 students and 1,500 full-time and 20,000 part-time faculty. Its overall graduation rate in 2010 was 16%.[3]

If you've spent years obtaining your PhD and worked in a research environment, you will find that most for-profit jobs are geared toward teaching only, with standardized course content you have little or no say about. You're a hired hand to teach what you're told to teach.

Should you become involved with them? Our first response is no (but see our next hint), certainly not as your first or second academic job. They'll pay much less than the not-for-profits. Working for one will do almost nothing for you professionally, and you won't have research time. In our opinion, the downside far exceeds the benefits.

35. Exceptions to the previous hint. If you're a graduate student who needs teaching experience or needs to supplement your munificent doctoral stipend, for-profit schools give you instant experience. Often your students are mature, older than you, and far more interested in your subject than 18- to 22-year-old undergraduates.

If you have your PhD in hand but not the academic job you long for, a for-profit can be a stopgap. It will supplement your unemployment insurance (if you're eligible) while giving you additional teaching experience. However, we have two caveats if you later want a permanent appointment in a not-for-profit:

- To be hired later by a school with a strong research requirement for its tenure track, keep your research going.
- For an appointment in a teaching institution, become an adjunct in a not-for-profit college to show you have teaching experience in that sector.

In either case, tell the not-for-profit's search committee you took the for-profit job to improve your teaching skills while looking for the right place to spend your career. Remember, not-for-profit faculty almost invariably look down their noses at the for-profits, in part because they compete with them.

36. Build a reference pool. To obtain a job (and tenure later) you will need references from beyond your dissertation committee. Build a reference pool; that is, identify people who will say nice things about you. They needn't be famous or distinguished, but they should hold impressive titles or be employed at prestigious places. References from abroad are particularly desirable since they show you to be a person with some international reputation in your field. Remember that universities are lazy. When they need references, they will ask you for a long list of names to choose from. Pick your friends.

37. RÉSUMÉS ARE IMPORTANT.[4] They are your entrée to the process. Invest in having yours done professionally. It should be neat but not gaudy. Include everything in your résumé that is remotely relevant. Some search committees use a checklist of skills, experiences, and other criteria they expect for a position. Do you know something about, say, medieval literature or databases, that the department might want you to teach? A committee may blindly drop you from consideration if its members don't put a checkmark next to each of their items. Your problem is that the list of items is different at every institution.

38. DUAL CAREERS. If you have a spouse or significant other with a career, you may incur obstacles to accepting a good offer. Dual careers usually mean that two jobs are needed. This situation is particularly difficult if the spouse is also an academic, and you require two appointments, say, in biochemistry and political science. In rare and usually senior cases, the university quickly approves a spousal hire. Most departments making an offer to one spouse will try to assist the second spouse in locating an academic appointment. But that is a tough game to play.

39. THE SHORT LIST. Search committees receive many more applications than they can deal with. They prefer to deal with just a few. Therefore, their usual procedure is to create a short list of candidates to consider further. To be on the short list, you need to stand out from the crowd.

The procedure varies from search to search. Sometimes the committee checks references before inviting a short-listed candidate to campus, sometimes after.[5] Sometimes committee members conduct interviews by phone before choosing whom to invite. So, in your application,

- don't be modest. Make sure your major achievements are highlighted in your résumé and in your cover letter.
- craft each cover letter carefully. It's shocking, but some search committee members read only the cover letters. Specify how your work relates to the requirements of the specific job.
- follow all instructions. Some committees winnow applicants by removing any application that omits anything they asked for, such as a statement about your philosophy of teaching.
- ask for your reference letters early. The main reason some applications are set aside is that the folder is incomplete because a reference you suggested is missing, even though that reference would have been top notch.

Once your application package is complete, proofread it (Hint 214). Tiny errors, like misspellings or a wrong date, can keep you off the short list.[6]

Job Opportunities

This section focuses on the types of employment opportunities available for new and recent PhDs beyond the usual academic appointments in a college or university. These options should help you in deciding which kinds of jobs to look for. The problem is one of information: your obtaining information about available jobs for yourself, and potential employers' obtaining information about you. The next twelve hints focus on your information needs. Remember, however, you want information about your availability to reach employers you haven't yet considered. An important way of doing so is making your résumé broadly accessible. For academic jobs, some professional societies compile collections of résumés of members (including student members) looking for employment and make them available to schools that are hiring in their members' specialties. Find out if this is true in your field. If you are seeking a new position, make sure you are on your professional society's list. Also, find out which professional meetings (Hints 193 and 194) include recruiting.

40. THE LAW OF SUPPLY AND DEMAND applies to academia as much as to other fields. You are playing a futures game on the job market, no different from a high roller in the stock market, when you select a field of study for your PhD. Since it takes four to seven years or more to acquire the degree, you make the assumption that your services will be in demand several years from now. That assumption may be true, but then again it may not be. Fields move in and out of favor over time. When a hot new field or specialty opens up, it is an exciting time. Lots of people wander in from adjacent fields. They form departments or concentration areas and begin training PhDs in that specialty. Skilled people are in short supply, and salary offers are good. However, what usually happens is that within a relatively short period of time, the PhD market becomes saturated, and jobs become scarcer. Furthermore, other new specialties emerge, and schools cut back on the previous fad. A classic example is operations research, also known as management science. In the 1960s new departments were formed. By the 1980s the job market was saturated. In the last decade supply exceeded demand, and this in a field that offers industrial as well as academic employment. The obvious implication for graduate students is that fields with an oversupply of applicants make it much harder to obtain either an initial job or tenure. Moreover, the academic prestige of the school that hires you will, on average, be lower—and so will the salary.

41. RESEARCH- VERSUS TEACHING-ORIENTED INSTITUTIONS. When job hunting, one of the first choices you make is whether to apply to teaching or to research institutions. The two types differ in that teaching schools require some research output, whereas research schools require lots of research output. Both require teaching skills.

Your choice depends on whether you think of yourself first as a teacher who does research or as a researcher who also teaches.

Research institutions are typically megauniversities.[7] If your field is part of science, technology, engineering, and mathematics (STEM), or similar areas supported by government and grant organizations, you will be expected to bring in research money to support your research, be involved in writing grant applications almost from the day you arrive, and be involved in the PhD program.

Teaching institutions want you to have a PhD to certify your intellectual ability to do research but do not insist that you be a research entrepreneur. However, the ability to obtain grants will help you with tenure and promotion.

42. THE JOBS MAY BE AT FOR-PROFIT INSTITUTIONS.[8] For-profit schools carry a large amount of baggage that makes them less attractive than not-for-profits for an academic job (Hint 34). In 2011–2012 the growth of academia is in the for-profit sector and may continue to be there. The argument about lack of growth in not-for-profits is by analogy. In 2006–2010, job growth among businesses five years old or more was zero. Furthermore, almost no not-for-profit, tenure-granting institutions opened then or are slated to open in the next two years.

Conclusion: Not-for-profit higher education is a mature industry. Most of the jobs involve replacing people who leave or retire. Yes, there is some regional growth, but it is offset by contraction elsewhere.

43. NEW PROGRAMS. Colleges, like businesses, respond to perceived demand by offering new programs. The programs may be a new school (e.g., law, pharmacy, nursing), a new department, or a new area in an existing department. The advantages of such programs are that they are not encumbered by their past, usually have more than one position available, and have a future. However, they are not risk-free. Sometimes subjects that seem to be leading edge or potential winners turn out not to be. If few students show up, the programs are canceled, and the people who were hired wind up back in job-hunting mode. If you land such a job, be aware that you will be expected to help set up the curriculum and the necessary infrastructure. That cuts into your research productivity and hence your ability to be hired elsewhere. Bottom line: you need to be careful and be willing to take the risk.

To find new programs, examine the employment ads in the *Chronicle of Higher Education* and the lists of new programs that appear from time to time on *Inside Higher Ed.*

44. NATIONAL RANKINGS. If, when considering places to send your job application, you take into account national rankings of schools and departments, be very careful. Rankings of universities and departments are strongly influenced by a halo effect. In a classic case several years ago, Penn State's law school was ranked well by law school deans. But there was one little problem: Penn State did not have a law school at that time.[9]

Measurement problems that plague, and often invalidate, such rankings include the following:

- A poorly ranked university may have the top-ranked department in your discipline while a highly ranked university may be mediocre in your discipline.

▪ Graduate programs, and universities, achieve status almost entirely through scholarly publications (or football teams), not through effective teaching. Graduate department ratings, and by implication overall university ratings, are profoundly affected by institutional and departmental size. The correlation is high between department ranking and the total number of articles by its faculty that are published in highly cited journals. The correlation is much lower when per-faculty publication rates are used. Naïve aspiring faculty candidates who apply to departments based on rank may be choosing large departments characterized by low levels of research and poor teaching.

Many institutions try to game the system to inflate their quality ratings. They know ranking organizations use variables that are easy to obtain and adjust accordingly. As a newly minted PhD or when changing jobs, you should focus not on rankings, but rather on your fit with a department and on whether the culture is supportive. The information you really need is given in the other hints in this chapter but is not usually reflected in published rankings.

Nonetheless, ratings for the school as a whole, not the department, affect your reputation and the quality levels of students you wind up teaching.

45. TEACHING IN A COMMUNITY COLLEGE. Doctoral students don't usually envision themselves as being in training for a position in a two-year community college. Yet, in a tight job market, and with skills in teaching, those completing the doctorate or with one already in-hand can consider these institutions a viable source of jobs.

Community colleges play an important role in our higher education system. They are engines of social mobility. Many talented students cannot afford to attend a four-year institution right out of high school. They plan to matriculate at their local community college for two years and then transfer. Other students seek advanced vocational or technical training and certification for well-paying jobs in our high-tech economy. Some of those students are reverse transfers, people with a bachelor's degree who seek specialized knowledge and skills leading to employment.

The prevalence of community colleges varies by states. In California, where we both live, over 100 are well established. In this state, and we suspect everywhere, a faculty position at a community college pays less than public four-year colleges or public universities with graduate programs.

Be aware of the trade-offs. Your teaching load will be heavy. However, the teaching can be challenging and fulfilling. You will not be encouraged to conduct research, but you can discipline yourself to conduct research and publish if your goal is to join a research institution.

46. ONLINE UNIVERSITIES. Online universities are proliferating, but range in quality. Some are highly questionable degree mills. Others are well-organized, accredited, respected academic organizations. An example of the latter category at the time this Hint was written is Walden University. Some online universities provide extensive training programs for new faculty, including discussion of teaching standards. Most online universities are for-profits (Hints 34 and 35).

47. THE ASSISTANT DEAN STRATEGY. If your field suffers from an oversupply of people, one strategy is to seek a job as an assistant dean. This approach is quite tricky. Colleges are always looking for candidates for such necessary but nonglorious jobs as assistant dean for student affairs or assistant dean of administration or assistant dean for summer school. You, as an applicant, should insist that you also receive an appointment (even if not tenure track) in your field of specialty, say, history. You should also insist that you teach one course and that you are given some time for research. Unless you do so, you will never be given a crack at a tenure-track position. You must then be active in your department and be seen by the department as a member in good standing who gives it access to the administration. Even then, you may never be fully accepted (see Hint 147 on joint appointments). However, you will gain experience that can be used later, and you will gain the academic title (and the teaching and research experience) needed on your résumé when you look for a job involving full-time teaching and research.

48. EVALUATE A POSTDOC CAREFULLY, particularly if you are in the sciences. You should think of a postdoc in cold, hard economic terms. It is an investment (or speculation, depending on your point of view) just like buying stocks or real estate. You will certainly be paid less than if you took a teaching position, but you may gain additional knowledge and experience to make more money in the long run in your chosen field. The anticipated benefits must exceed the short-run costs to make the investment worthwhile. A postdoc is appropriate under the following conditions:

- You are in a field where jobs at good places are scarce and you did not get one, or you failed to follow Hint 31 and delayed starting your job search for too long.
- You feel you need to gain specific research tools (or, if you're a scientist, experience with specialized equipment) to be able to move your research past your PhD dissertation.
- You want to work with a specific individual (preferably one of the powerful 100; see Hint 2) who will further your growth.
- You want to build up your publication list without using up your seven-year tenure clock.

A postdoc is not appropriate if you are afraid of teaching or talking in front of people. You are merely delaying the inevitable: rejection. See Hint 74 for help. A postdoc is also not appropriate if you are tired of living on a shoestring for years while working on your PhD or need to support a family.

49. NONACADEMIC OPPORTUNITIES. You may find as you go through your job search that you don't really want to work in academe, or you may be one of the unlucky ones who doesn't find the right assistant professorship or postdoc or assistant dean's job. In that case, you start to think in terms of finding other employment. The classic case was that of Albert Einstein:

> His impudence and lack of deference to authority . . . alienated all of his professors at Zurich Polytechnic. . . . He was the only graduate in his section . . . not offered a junior professorship.[10]

It made his career. A job was found for him at the Swiss Patent Office that gave him time away from the pressures of meeting classes and grinding out research papers so that he could think. The result was the theory of relativity and much more. Eventually, he was invited to become a professor.

The point of this story is that innovation and creativity can be gained outside an academic career as much as inside. When you achieve the PhD degree, it is a point of discontinuity in your life when many alternative paths are open to you. The tenure track is only one of them. Life, after all, is what you make of it.

50. NONUNIVERSITY RESEARCH ORGANIZATIONS offer the challenge of research without the need or the opportunity to teach. They include industry laboratories, major consulting firms, government laboratories, and not-for-profit think tanks. Each organization has its distinct culture. Many involve military work. In the not-for-profits and the consulting firms, you are only as good as the last contract you brought in. As a result, these organizations experience a high burnout rate among people 45 or older. If you want to go back to academia at some time in the future, you need to create your own portable wealth by publishing (Hint 70). Unfortunately, publishing is counter to the culture of many of these organizations. In some industrial laboratories it is said that even if you write $F = ma$ or $E = mc^2$, someone will stamp your report "Company Confidential."

51. TEACHING OVERSEAS FOR FUN AND PROFIT. You can become involved in teaching overseas in several ways. Here are a few.

- Your institution runs an overseas program and asks you to teach in it for a semester or a year.
- You are hired specifically by a college to teach overseas.
- You are hired by an institution in another country.
- You receive a Fulbright or other grant that includes overseas teaching.

Advantages: If you're interested in the country or have relatives there, you can visit them with your travel expenses paid, and you can travel in the region at a much lower cost than if you started from the United States. If your research involves the country, you can do it there. You can familiarize yourself with foreign cultures and attend overseas conferences. You will develop a broader outlook and make new friends.

Disadvantages: You probably will not be able to do much research while away. If untenured, you lose time on your clock (Hint 126), unless you can arrange to stop the clock while away. You incur costs at both ends (e.g., shutting down your home in the United

States while having uncompensated living expenses at your home abroad).

Bottom line: Weigh the benefits and the costs. Investigate the economics involved, and try not to wind up subsidizing the experience.

Interviewing

Once you've applied for a position and made it to the short list, you will be asked to come to campus for an interview. In addition to reading this set of hints, also read the ones on data gathering, because some of that data is best gathered during your interview.

52. Tactics for interviewing. You may start out self-confidently on your first interview assuming you can wing it, or you may be so timid that you just know you're going to fail. In either case, you will run into portions of the interview that go like a charm and other parts that don't. Fortunately, almost everybody gets more than one interview. Just like teaching (Hint 72), being interviewed is a learned art.

Remember: You are going to accept only one job, but you will (hopefully) be interviewed by many. You will have to deal with rejection, but you most likely learned how to do that when you applied to multiple graduate schools.

The secret to landing a job is to try for many and not be intimidated or crushed by rejections, which are inevitable. You will likely lose out on many job competitions before you finally land a good position.

The most important part of interviewing as a finalist for an academic position is the "job talk," which is usually a lecture about your research. Prepare your presentation carefully. Rehearse it, preferably in front of friends. Ask for their comments and criticisms.[11]

53. DRESSING FOR THE JOB INTERVIEW. With a tough job market, a lot depends on the initial interview. The initial, and later, interview outcomes often depend on the impression you make when you walk into the room. Don't turn people off before you even start talking. All the interviewers know about you is in the résumé you sent and how you look. The adage "clothes make the person" is still true.

Admittedly if you are a graduate student who lived hand-to-mouth for years, dressed in a wardrobe of jeans and Birkenstocks, you may not have the right clothes in your closet. If you don't, go to local clothes outlets or even thrift shops and use a credit card if necessary. Make sure the clothes fit. This investment pays off.

54. DON'T BE INTIMIDATED BY THE SCHOOLS YOUR INTERVIEWERS ATTENDED. Before interviewing at a particular institution, look in the catalog to find out where faculty received their doctorates. Don't be fooled by the names of the schools. Even top schools graduate mediocre people who do nothing once they are anointed with a PhD. Conversely, others are world-class scholars who would be delightful colleagues but may have attended no-name institutions.

Be discriminating. You want to work with pleasant people who have good ideas, a good work ethic, and who value honesty and cooperation.

Here are some warning signs to help you decide about the people you meet at the interview. Be wary of interviewers who:

1. use a three-syllable word when one syllable will do;
2. make too big a deal out of the school named on their PhD;
3. give you the sense you can't trust them;
4. disparage their colleagues;
5. ask intrusive personal questions, such as about your relationship status or your age (both are illegal);

6. have phony British accents and sound like an Oxford don; and
7. hang unimpressive plaques on the wall. They are impressive only if they are for solid achievements, for example, being editor of a journal, presenting the best paper at a meeting, or for teaching excellence. They're not impressive if they recognize speaking at a local Kiwanis meeting or at a seminar at a nearby school five years ago.

55. INTERVIEW YOUR POTENTIAL BOSSES (e.g., chair, dean) while they interview you. You will live rather intimately with them for a long time. Make sure you are compatible.

56. DEALING WITH INTERVIEWERS WHO HAVE PUBLISHED LESS THAN YOU HAVE. If you are a new PhD or an active researcher, many if not most of the senior people who interview you probably produced less research in the last three years than you did. This is particularly true for older faculty who were granted tenure in easier times. When you are interviewed by such people, be kind. Stress the importance of your research but don't overwhelm them with the details. You don't want them to perceive you as a threat to the comfortable positions they now hold.

57. PREPARE AN ELEVATOR SPEECH. Throughout your PhD studies, your professors grounded you in your discipline and taught you how to disclose all the caveats and disclaimers that must accompany your scholarly research. Then, in the dissertation defense and afterward—for example, when you seek a job—you are asked to succinctly summarize your work and what it means.

Prepare an elevator speech. Imagine you are attending a national conference. You step into an express elevator on the 45th floor of the building and push the lobby button. The only other person in the elevator is, say, the senior federal policymaker in your area of interest, someone from the National Endowment for the Humanities, the U.S. president's science adviser, or the chair of the department where you really want to interview for a job. She heard you completed an important dissertation study and would like to know about your research. Because of a packed schedule, she only has this elevator ride available to learn about your work. What do you tell her?

Data Gathering

In addition to gathering data about potential employers before you submit an application, you will be gathering data during and after the interview to help you decide whether you want to be part of that institution if they make you an offer.

58. DETERMINE THE CULTURES. In large institutions, school and department cultures will differ, ranging from cooperative to cutthroat. Often the culture will change when a new person is appointed president or provost or dean or department chair. That is what makes these appointments so critical to the quality of your life. A cooperative culture should be treasured. It will help you as a young faculty member. Conversely, a cutthroat culture is particularly stressful for young faculty if they arrive not knowing the culture of the place and are unprepared to handle it. When interviewing, try to find out whether the members of the faculty like one another, and try to assess the cultural norms from what they tell you. Asking graduate students about faculty infighting won't help because they are usually insulated from it. Remember that in addition to trying to assess your capabilities and fit with their needs, the interviewers are trying to present as good a picture of themselves as they can so you will accept their offer should they make one. Thus, always assume that actual conditions are much worse than they are painted during the interview. If you are lucky enough to receive multiple offers, investigate the cultures involved in your choice by speaking with those you know at the school and with those who recently left it.

59. GATHER SALARY AND TENURE DATA. These are the two pieces of data about an institution that are most important to you. Ask yourself,

1. am I being offered the right amount of money?
2. what are the chances of my achieving tenure?

To answer the first question, obtain information on the salary levels for people in your field. The American Association of University Professors publishes salary averages for many (but not all) colleges. See Chapter 9 for more on salaries.

60. OBTAINING INFORMATION ON TENURE LEVELS IS A LITTLE TRICKIER. First, the number of tenure cases per year in an academic unit tends to be small. You need data for your specialty. However, knowing the tenure fraction for the institution as a whole is also important. If a school tenures 1 in 10, it is a far different place from one that tenures 8 in 10. Just knowing success percentages in the tenure process is not enough. Some schools weed out at the three-year point. Others make tenure so tough that faculty self-destruct by resigning early. Talk with people who recently made tenure in the department They will usually have the best view of the current situation.

61. ASK ABOUT THE RETIREMENT SYSTEM. It is really not too early to worry about retirement when interviewing for your first job because it can affect your mobility economically from then on. You will most likely be in a state retirement system or in the Teachers

Insurance and Annuity Association–College Retirement Equities Fund (TIAA–CREF) retirement system. TIAA–CREF is subscribed to by most private and some public institutions. In TIAA–CREF, once vested (these days, it's usually at once) you keep what you have when you move to another institution. State retirement plans are portable within the state but not from one state to another. The major problem comes when you move from a TIAA–CREF college to a state institution or the other way around.

For more about retirement, see Hint 142.

62. PARKING.

> The chancellor's job had come to be defined as providing parking for the faculty, sex for the students, and athletics for the alumni.
>
> –Clark Kerr, chancellor of the University of California, Berkeley, 1957

Be sure to inquire about parking, because parking can be a big deal. For example, at the University of California the joke is that the university is really a parking business that runs its ten campuses as a way to attract customers. Unless you wind up living a short walk or bike ride from your campus office or living in a city with decent public transportation with stops near your home and your campus, you have little choice but to drive to work. If you do, you may be charged a parking fee, usually deducted from your pay. The deduction is from your gross pay and is therefore taxable at your top rate just as your Social Security contribution. Whether you pay a fee or not, all you get is a hunting license to find a space. Some schools do offer reserved parking at an increased fee, which means that a space is available but not the same one every day. The top fee can be substantial; $750 a year for a reserved space is not uncommon. You can't do much about parking costs except to carpool. But carpooling is difficult because you need to find people who live near you and who are on campus at the same times you are. Be sure to include parking costs in analyzing the true income associated with an offer.

63. DETERMINE REAL PAY. Don't assume that the only relevant dollar number associated with an offer is the total salary. It isn't. What you most need to know is how much money you can spend, how much the spending money can buy, and the quality of life associated with the offer. Here are some considerations:

- Cost of housing. The cost is greater and house sizes are smaller in, say, Los Angeles than they are in Cedar Falls, Iowa.
- Cost of living other than housing. College towns and big cities are generally more expensive to live in but offer more amenities such as theater and cultural and sports activities.
- Quality of schools for your children. Most places, other than college towns, overestimate their schools in their official estimates.
- Local tax structure for sales, state income, and real estate taxes. Yes, you will make enough money that you need to worry about taxes.
- Availability of work for your spouse in the community. Like those who overestimate school quality, the people hiring you will overestimate the availability of jobs for spouses.
- The cost of campus parking. Use the current year for your estimate. Parking costs usually tend to increase slowly.

Offers

64. GET THE OFFER IN WRITING, READ IT, AND NEGOTIATE BEFORE YOU ACCEPT. Usually, once you are selected by a search committee, you receive the offer over the phone. The phone conversation typically includes the salary offered, what your title will be, and a few other details. You will be pressed to make a decision quickly (sometimes on the spot), because if you decline, the school will offer the position to its backup candidate. We recommend you find out about the details of the offer and negotiate if necessary before you accept.[12]

Get the offer in writing, including all the detailed promises that were made and agreed to. Not only do you want the job, but the institution has decided you are the one. They want you badly. Be aware that the administrators who make the offer may, and often do, lie. The severity of their memory loss when you arrive on campus can far exceed anything that could be reasonably expected at their stage of life. If you disagree with them, they tell you that there must have been a misunderstanding. As we said, get it in writing.

You will find details about your work life throughout this book, ranging from teaching loads to computing support to research time to parking. Make a list of what is critical for you (see Hint 67). Then obtain clarifications and agreements in writing about items not in the offer. If things get sticky, you may need to hire a lawyer. Only then sign the contract.

65. GET YOUR PHD BEFORE YOU START THE TENURE TRACK, UNLESS YOU ARE STARVING OR HOMELESS. Don't take a tenure-track faculty position without the PhD in hand. If you do, we estimate the odds are two to one against your ever finishing your degree. Even if you do finish while on the job, your chances of being tenured go down because you reduced the seven-year clock (see Hint 126). Furthermore, without a PhD you will be offered a significantly lower salary, and you may never make up the difference. If you must work, the only defense you have is to negotiate with the institution that the clock does not start ticking until you can legitimately be called "Doctor."

66. AVOID TAKING YOUR FIRST JOB AT A SCHOOL YOU ATTENDED, no matter how strong your alumni loyalty. You will always be regarded as a graduate student by the older faculty and will be treated as such. It is different, however, if you leave for some years and then return.

67. CHOOSING AMONG OFFERS. Your lifestyle is a prime consideration in your job search. Create a table listing what is important to you and how each offer matches your list. The list provides guidance about what to look for in your job hunt. You may want to prepare this list (see Hint 64) before you go on the market.

Decide which offer comes closest to the way you (and your family) want to live over the years that follow. Remember, no institution will be perfect.

Just picking the offer with the larger nine-month salary is much too simplistic. The government's consumer price index (CPI) is an indicator of how far the money will go in a particular location. For example, the New York City CPI is high, but transportation is cheap. In Los Angeles the CPI is lower, but you must own a car and drive a lot. Housing prices are high in both places but low in rural settings. Evaluate in terms of your lifestyle.

Ignore small differences in the salary offered. A $1,000-a-year difference comes down to about $20 a week.

Examine benefits such as health insurance and retirement contributions, among others—for example, travel allowances (Hint 192), computer support, sabbatical leave (Hint 150), and tuition remission for your children. Benefits can be quite different among offers.

Quality-of-life issues also include school systems, airport access, climate, and the availability of your favorite type of entertainment, be it symphony, theater, country dancing, or hunting.

Hunting for the Next Job

68. POSITIONING YOURSELF FOR THE NEXT JOB. Professors, like everyone else, make mistakes. You may find you have great qualms about the job you took and desperately want to get out. It may be that you found the lifestyle suffocating or your colleagues unbearable or the students unprepared for your subject or your significant other desperately unhappy or the school deciding to fire you after three years. Whatever the cause, you want to restart your life in a new institution. In this moment of panic you need to think through what to do with the rest of your life. Here are some suggestions.

1. Be discreet. Don't go around telling everyone how bad life is. The people you work with are mostly happy and they don't want to hear about it. Certainly don't badmouth the institution or leave in a huff. You want to leave amicably so that you receive decent recommendations. Remember, tenured academics have long memories and are around for a considerable time.

2. You are back at square one, where you were when you received your PhD. The job-hunting steps are the same:
    a. Update your résumé and record everything you've accomplished since your degree.
    b. Check for advertised available openings. Attend conferences where recruiting occurs.
    c. Circulate your résumé.

3. Tell your mentor(s) and people you know and trust that you would like to move. They know you, and most of them will want to help. They will tip you off about positions that might fit you. If any are one of the 100 powerful people in the field (Hint 2), so much the better.

4. You can be general about your reasons for leaving and couch them in terms of looking for new opportunities. Be aware that

even if you try to keep your desire to move quiet, leaks occur, some of which inevitably reach your institution. If you have a boss who believes that even thinking of leaving their Land of Eden is treason, be prepared for trouble.

5. It is easier to move to a school that is lower in the pecking order than higher. Administrators at mid-level schools like to brag that they hired from the Ivy League and so on down the line. Horizontal moves do occur sometimes, but only for those with an impressive record.

6. The best position is when you are approached by someone from an institution better or equal to yours. Unfortunately, that situation is infrequent, even if you have special talents in a hot area.

69. IF YOU BECOME UNEMPLOYED. People in academia do lose their jobs. They are fired, not tenured, their department is eliminated, or they quit. If it happens to you, you are suddenly back to where you were before you received your PhD.

Unemployment is not trivial. You may not be eligible for unemployment insurance. Even if you are, government insurance pays much less than your current salary. You stand to lose benefits such as health insurance. Unless you are independently wealthy (and few academics are), you need employment and you need it quickly.

Fortunately, unless you quit on the spur of the moment in a huff in the middle of a semester, you have some time between when you know you need a job and when your paycheck stops. Use that time to move back into employment. Some things you can do:

- To stay in academia, search the job openings in the *Chronicle of Higher Education* and *Inside Higher Ed.* You may have to move to a lower-ranking institution or teach at a for-profit school (Hint 35).

- Consider temporary one-year visiting professor appointments and assistant deanships.
- Accept adjunct teaching appointments in other institutions within travel distance. We don't recommend adjunct appointments that require moving unless you are in a small, isolated college town with no local options.
- Complete a book that offers a decent advance against royalties. However, this arrangement is easier said than done.
- Investigate nonprofit and for-profit nonacademic organizations that require skills you have, such as translating a foreign language, or knowledge of statistics or finance. Some firms won't touch a PhD (overqualified), while others like the idea of a PhD on their staff.

In many situations you may need to move, which is more difficult if you have a working spouse (Hint 38).

Notes

1. Neither of us ever worked for a for-profit educational organization. Our opinions are based on what we've observed over the last decade.

2. For the results of this survey, see http://www.gao.gov/new.items/d10948t.pdf

3. Ibid.

4. Résumés are sometimes called *curriculum vitae, vita, vitae,* and *CV* in academia. Although slightly different, the terms are used interchangeably. Note that *vita* is singular and *vitae* is plural.

5. Sometimes, however, you are asked to include reference letters with your application.

6. See Woolf, E. (2010, October 13). "Standing out from the herd." *Inside Higher Ed.* Retrieved from http://www.insidehighered.com/advice/on_the_fence/woolf7.

7. For example, the authors' institution, Claremont Graduate University, is a self-standing PhD-granting research institution, albeit a small one.

Some PhD-granting departments are parts of small universities, which is the exception rather than the rule.

8. Dean Dad, "Startups," *Confessions of a Community College Dean* (blog), December 9, 2010, http://app3.insidehighered.com/blogs/confes sions_of_a_community_college_dean/startups.

9. M. Gladwell, "The Order of Things," *The New Yorker*, February 14, 2011, 68–75.

10. Walter Isaacson. (2007, April 12). Einstein's theory of creativity the wellspring of future genius. *The Sydney Morning Herald*. Retrieved from http://www.smh.com.au/news/opinion/einsteins-theory-of-creativity-the-wellspring-of-future-genius/2007/04/11/1175971177263.html.

11. For more details on interview tactics, see Wright, T. (2010, October 27). If I could do it over. *Inside Higher Ed*. Retrieved from http://www .insidehighered.com/advice/2010/10/27/wright.

12. An example of what you need to negotiate is a publication subvention when you publish your dissertation as a book. Some publishers charge the author for costly items (e.g., color), and all require the author to obtain copyright permissions. Sums in the thousands of dollars can be involved. You're more likely to get the school to agree to provide the funds on the way in, rather than after you accept the offer and arrive on campus.

5

TEACHING

HINT 75: MEETING CLASSES IS PARAMOUNT. . . . . Students are very conscious of the amount of money they spend for your class.

ALL FACULTY MEMBERS, whether at a teaching or a research institution, spend a considerable portion of their lives in the classroom and involved in service that helps govern the institution. Teaching is a fundamental condition for staying in academe. Furthermore, you may find that teaching and mentoring provide some of your most rewarding professional experiences. You have the opportunity to make a positive impact on your students' careers and lives.

70. PUBLICATIONS ARE THE ONLY FORM OF PORTABLE WEALTH. Teaching is a great personal satisfaction and is an important public good that you perform. It is an important, necessary condition, but not a sufficient one for being hired or tenured.

71. MANY COLLEGES AND UNIVERSITIES VALUE TEACHING. Some people want to become professors, love to teach, and believe research is a necessary evil to get their ticket punched. Without publishing, it is impossible to receive tenure in most schools, particularly in research universities. Happily, however, the pendulum is swinging. Many colleges and even some universities now value teaching and reward it on its own merits. But you better be a superteacher.

72. TEACHING IS A LEARNED ART. As such it follows a learning curve. Your first effort will not be as good as your second, and your second, not as good as your third. However, there is a limit on how good you will get. In other words, your teaching ratings will peak and then remain essentially constant. Eventually you will be bored by the course, and your teaching ratings will go down. Don't despair. It is a natural phenomenon. Often, it is a result of aging; faculty over 40 relate less and less each year to 18-year-old freshmen if they don't have kids at home anymore. Decreasing teaching ratings are a signal that it is time for you to teach a different course or students at a different level. You may need to strong-arm your department chair, but change you must.

73. Being a mentor. Strive to be a good mentor as well as a good teacher. The difference between the two terms is subtle, but important. *Mentoring* almost always refers to guiding one student in his or her studies and career planning.

Mentoring is a key component of your responsibilities if you work with PhD students and, to a lesser degree, if you work with master's or undergraduate students. If you do mentoring well, you create friends for life. Years from now you will inevitably conclude that your most important and most personally satisfying professional contributions came from mentoring.

Take the mentoring responsibility seriously. Commit time and energy to guiding your mentees. If you had a helpful mentor, think carefully about how he or she helped you. In addition to the theories, models, literature, and analytical techniques you impart, take time to help your protégés get over intellectual hurdles, and tell them about the practical aspects of career development. Make students aware of the choices they face and the associated pros and cons. Don't make decisions for them; give them the information they need to make wise choices.

Learn how to improve your teaching and mentoring from the extensive literature about college teaching, teaching in general, and on mentoring.[1]

74. Go to Toastmasters International if you need tips on how to be entertaining and informative in front of a group of students (www.toastmasters.org). We have seen it work in many cases. Ignore the fact that Toastmasters attracts mostly business people; the environment gives you privacy from your colleagues.

75. MEETING CLASSES IS PARAMOUNT. Don't cancel classes. For example, if you are out of town attending a national scholarly meeting on a class day, arrange for a colleague to cover for you or arrange a makeup time with the class. If you know far enough in advance when you will be out of town, you can schedule an examination on that day, and be sure it is proctored properly. Missing classes creates more ill will from students than anything else you do. If you miss a lot of classes, even if they are covered by someone else, students will resent you for it. Students assume they are taking the class from you, not from a collection of substitutes. In high-tuition institutions (and even in some modest ones) students are very conscious of the amount of money they spend for your class. They will take it out on you on your class ratings. They will complain to the department chair and your colleagues. You will also pile up debts to colleagues you must repay by covering their classes for them. If you have to repay many such debts, you will lose valuable time from your research and thus from your tenure clock.

76. TEACHING CAN BE A DANGEROUS PROFESSION. It doesn't happen very often, but a student (or a faculty member) can come into your office or your building and shoot at you or cause other physical harm. The 2007 tragedy at Virginia Tech, where a student shot and killed 33 people including himself, is a poignant example. More often than not, these incidents are associated with a student failing a class or having a grievance. These admittedly rare tragedies introduce workplace risk to the academic profession. As stated in Hint 152, as a faculty member you are a public person. Your actions affect the lives of real people. Students are prone to the same mental disturbances as people in the society as a whole. A few may be sufficiently unbalanced to take harmful action.

You can reduce your risk by learning about aberrant behavior (e.g., talk to the psychology staff at your campus health service) and by reporting your concerns to the health service or campus police. Be aware of your campus's policy and don't try to solve the problem on your own. You may become a target.

77. CONSIDER COSTS TO STUDENTS WHEN SELECTING TEXTBOOKS. Perhaps the least considered factor that goes into the selection of a text for a course is its cost. Admittedly, you have no choice when teaching one or more sections of a standard multisection course whose text is selected by a committee or a course coordinator. However, when you alone make the choice, cost should be one of the criteria in your selection.

78. DON'T LET COMMITTEE WORK ERODE YOUR COMMITMENT TO TEACHING AND MENTORING. Regardless of the balance you strike between research and teaching, be careful not to let your faculty committee work crowd out the time planned to devote to either. Yes, the third major obligation of a professor is service, your contributions as a citizen of your institution. But be careful. Some committees chew up a lot of your time (Hints 183 and 184).

In the Classroom

79. SUMMARIES LOCK IN THE MATERIAL.[2] Save time at the end of a lecture for a clear, succinct summary of what you presented. Ask yourself, what key points should your students remember? Similarly, begin each class with a summary of what you presented in the previous session. At times, the short-term memory of distracted undergraduates (Hint 93) is as unreliable as that of some senior citizens. They need to be reminded what happened on Tuesday.

80. ENCOURAGE QUESTIONS. Establish ground rules about questions. The students should ask them when they have them, not wait silently for 15 minutes until it is "question time." If a student is confused by a concept, he or she will become totally lost in a subsequent discussion that builds on a concept unless you clarify it right then. However, students also should raise their hand when they have a question and wait for you to call on them. Do not answer questions that are shouted out, especially, "What did you just say?" Of course, if the students do that often enough they're telling you that your voice or their hearing is going.

81. ENJOY YOUR CLASSES. Presumably, you selected your field because you find it interesting and enjoyable. Many students accept that they should, or must, master your subject—such as statistics or opera—but consider it odious. Make the material come alive for them the way it does for you. You can teach statistics with gambling examples. The plots for the great operas make soap operas and police procedurals look tame by comparison. One colleague encountered high school students who said they hated math. "You like money, don't you?" he asked. "Of course," they replied. "Well, making money is all about math. Let me show you how."

82. LECTURING VERSUS FACILITATING. Faculty who spend their class time lecturing and faculty who prefer facilitating appear to be in a constant state of tension. This and the previous hints discuss lecturing, whereas the next hint discusses facilitation.

In the classical model of lecturing the faculty member walks into the classroom, opens the textbook or sets up the PowerPoint projector, and proceeds to drone on until the bell mercifully rings or the prepared material ends so the class can be dismissed early. This rigid caricature does not reflect what a good lecturer does.

Before discussing how to lecture, it is worth asking: why lecture at all? We contend that the course in which pure lecture or pure facilitation is the right approach is rare. Most undergraduate and graduate students don't know enough about a course's subject when they attend its first meeting to be able to discuss much more than what they saw on their social network or looked up on Wikipedia. They haven't read the textbook or the literature. They don't know what the issues are, or even why some ideas are issues at all.

83. TEACHING IS NOT SYNONYMOUS WITH LECTURING. Increasingly, professors are encouraged to be the "guide on the side," not the "sage on the stage." A growing literature deals with ways to engage students and to facilitate their learning above and beyond the traditional lecture, including class discussions and group projects. Try some of these other modes of teaching. Read about innovative pedagogical strategies.

Find an effective combination of strategies that seems to work for you. The approaches you select have to work for your personality. Furthermore, the relative value of a lecture versus, say, group discussion varies by discipline.

84. LECTURE CAPTURE. The electronic gizmos being sold to help teaching at the college level keep increasing, with one or two important new gadgets seeming to pop up every year. In 2011, as we wrote this second edition, electronic lecture capture was the rage.

Electronic lecture capture refers to recording a lecture or a class discussion so students can watch the lecture at their convenience on their own computer or at the library. The digital library where the lectures are stored might also contain slides, quizzes, and summaries.

Students are charged for using this material, and companies make money from them. The fees may be on a per-course basis, or if the institution buys the system for all courses, the fees are wrapped into a tuition increase. Publishers view lecture capture as a natural extension of their textbook market.

Whether lecture capture improves learning remains to be determined. Whether lecture capture will be used to increase class sizes, reduce the number of faculty required, or reduce most students to essentially taking courses online even though they are registered for face-to-face classes is not known.

Two important questions for prospective and young faculty:

- Who owns the lecture's intellectual property? With lecture capture you can be cloned many times over (or even sold to other institutions) and receive nothing for—as they're called in the entertainment business—the residual rights.
- What is the potential payoff for you? Your reputation could grow as a wider range of students view your lectures and are impressed by them.

85. OBTAINING STUDENT RESPONSES THROUGH TECHNOLOGY (CLICKERS[3]). If you want to know whether your students understand what you just described, or if you want their opinion, pose a question (typically true/false or multiple choice) and ask them to use their clickers (or texting) to respond.

The clicker technology is simple, yet it allows you to monitor student progress and stimulate productive discussions. Feedback is displayed quickly. Students will participate, especially if you set up the system so they know their individual responses are not revealed to other students.

Advantages: Student feedback is collected quickly (important in large courses), anonymity in class avoids stigma if students give the wrong answer, and, you can analyze individual responses later to find out who is learning and who is not.

Clickers provide a reality check and, often, a teachable moment. The trick is to create questions that stimulate thinking. If almost all students give the right answer, you can proceed. If most answers are wrong, go back and explain some more. Including common misconceptions in the possible answers can lead to discussions for clarification if too many students choose the misconceptions.

86. POWERPOINT PRESENTATIONS. PowerPoint is a powerful visual complement to lecturing. The software is user-friendly, visuals are easy to create, and students are accustomed to it. PowerPoint is most powerful when the text is sparse and primarily serves as a reminder.

Putting detailed information in your PowerPoint presentations loses your audience. They will not be listening to you because after studying the details displayed, they will spend their time copying the text in their notebooks. If you simply read what is on each PowerPoint slide, the students will tune you out.

Prepare paper versions of your PowerPoint slides (typically six to a page) for distribution. They provide a backup if the technology fails. If the technology works perfectly, hand out the paper version after your lecture. Otherwise, you may find yourself talking to the tops of their heads as they study the papers in front of them. For students, the paper version serves as a record, consulted at exam time. Just go to a school cafeteria before an exam and you will find students studying the handouts or using them to test one another.

If you are dissatisfied with PowerPoint, alternative presentation software is available on the market.

Teaching Online

87. DISTANCE EDUCATION refers to courses offered over the Internet to remotely located students rather than face-to-face in the classroom. The earliest such courses used television transmission of live classes to people in local industry. Remote students could respond and ask questions via a voice link. Today these courses use the Internet. They range from audio courses available on demand, to courses at fixed times with instructors present, to two-way video conferencing. The greater the richness of the medium, the greater the cost. Online is an increasing option for students. In 2009, for example, 5.6 million college and graduate students (29%) took at least one online course.[4]

Online is a much more intense way of teaching. It can require

- more time to prepare;
- more time in individual student contacts (often around the clock because they can be overseas);
- dealing with a broader range of student skills, intelligence, and maturity;
- good to excellent Internet skills; and
- great patience.

To understand what is involved with teaching online, talk with experienced faculty at your institution and observe one of more of their classes.

88. DISTANCE LEARNING IS A BLESSING AND A THREAT. It is a blessing because you can reach students who would otherwise not have the opportunity to learn from you or to savor the beauties of your field. It is a threat because college and university administrators might learn that it is cheaper to buy the infrastructure for distance learning than to construct new buildings or to hire new faculty. With distance learning you can instruct (some would say distract) hundreds simultaneously, not just the 10 or 30 in your classroom. Also, if you are not a superteacher on video or the Internet, you may not find much of a future market for your services even if you are a great researcher.

Students

89. BE WARY OF STUDENT EXCUSES. The death rate among aunts and grandmothers of college-age students is phenomenal, far beyond actuarial reality. It increases as exam time approaches. Although some students are remarkably inventive at concocting stories for this standard excuse for missing classes and exams, most are not. Faced with such an excuse, be aware that the student may be working you. These excuses can also snowball: if one student gets away with it, others follow, and you face a veritable epidemic of death among your student's relatives.

90. BELIEVE IT OR NOT, CHEATING IS WIDESPREAD at some undergraduate institutions. If you give tests (e.g., if you use the Scantron objective testing forms favored at many colleges), prepare alternative forms and interweave them throughout the class. Thus, each student who gets form A, on which column 2 would be the correct answer to the first question, is bracketed by two people who receive form B, on which column 4 would be the correct answer. Reproduce forms A and B on different colored paper, since students have been known to switch exams. If you are color blind, make sure the copying staff does not use both red and green paper.

91. TEACH EVERY STUDENT. As an educator, your goal should be to lead each and every student to master your subject.

Do not approach your work with the attitude that the material is difficult, only a few of them are intelligent enough to understand it, and you can't be concerned with the rest.

Don't assume that some students cannot learn the material, even advanced technical content, because they lack the aptitude or intelligence. Such judgments almost always are incorrect. Furthermore, they create a destructive self-fulfilling prophecy. If you believe that women can't learn advanced multivariate statistics (which is incorrect), or that a certain student is just not smart enough, that will color your instruction, your reactions to the student's questions or comments, and your evaluations of his or her work.

92. TEACH TO THE STUDENT'S FRAME OF REFERENCE. Learn as much as you can about each student's prior educational experiences, particularly in your discipline; his or her work experience; and hobbies or leisure interests. Consider asking about educational and professional experience in a carefully structured first assignment (but stop short of asking intrusive personal questions).

Later, try to frame answers to a student's questions with metaphors and examples he or she can relate to. For a nurse or nursing student, use medical metaphors. For an athlete, use sports metaphors. For a political science major, use examples from politics, say, in another country. Local or national politics in the United States can be tricky because the student's political views may be far different from yours.

By learning from the experiences and perspectives your students bring to the table, you will enrich your own understanding of your field.

93. DISTRACTED STUDENTS. As a new instructor, you will expect to see a sea of eager faces of students who listen to your every word and take copious notes. You may be surprised. You will see students dunking doughnuts and reading the campus newspaper or talking to each other or fondling each other or zoned out listening to their iPods. And what are they really watching on their laptops? Remember, your students, like you, grew up watching television. They forget that you can see them.

What to do about laptops and earphones? Our advice is laptops during lectures are acceptable. Earphones and zoning out to music that block out the lecture are not. Furthermore, we recommend banning laptops and cell phones during tests. It's too easy to communicate about the test via e-mail or texting, and cell phones can be used to photograph the test.

94. UNDERGRADUATES DON'T RECALL MUCH FROM SEVEN OR MORE YEARS AGO. We all use stories from our past to make a point in class. The stories humanize the material and increase student interest. However, if the stories are too old, 18- to 22-year-old undergraduates won't know what you're talking about. Examples are movies, books, references to events (particularly events abroad), old computer technologies, or software. If it happened seven or more years ago, it is beyond their recollections. The period of recall is a little longer for older students and graduate students.

95. WILL THIS BE ON THE FINAL? Many students, especially undergraduates, are totally focused on their grades and maximizing their GPAs. They are grade grubbing. Such students measure themselves by the grades they receive. They see themselves as being worth more than you or others see them. Be it a failing student who thinks he deserves a B, or an A minus student who doesn't understand why she didn't receive at least an A if not an A plus, the story is almost always the same: "You don't see true worth when it is in front of you" and "I worked so hard in this course and was there every day, so I deserve an A." What they don't see is that the grade is a measure of output, not input. All they know about is their own work. You know what they produced in writing or said in class. The stories can be plaintive and even heart wrenching. Don't cave. The word will spread and the cases will multiply.

A key grade grubbing indicator shows up on the first day of class. We are very specific on what different parts of a course are worth, and we include that information in the syllabus. We identify grade grubbers by the inordinate number of questions they ask about something simple in the syllabus. When these very students receive disappointing test or assignment grades, they swear they never saw the rules in the syllabus.

If you said, "As I was walking from the parking lot to the classroom, I passed a burning bush. A voice from above spoke to me and told me the meaning of life," a student in the front row would surely ask, "Will this be on the final?"

Of course, students never ask you to reduce their grade.

96. GRADE INFLATION. U.S. undergraduate grades rose substantially over the last six decades, particularly at selective and private colleges.[5] The data show that at these institutions the mean GPA went up about 0.1 point per decade, from 2.52 in the 1950s to 3.11 in 2006–2007. The study indicates that students' mean grade point average is highly dependent on an institution's student quality and whether the school is private or public.

Although the data are clear, their causes are in dispute. Is it caused by faculty fear of student evaluations? Do faculty want to give good students a leg up in grad school admissions? Does grade inflation in high schools lead students to expect better grades in college? Are adjuncts giving higher grades so they don't lose their jobs? Are today's students really smarter?

The data imply that you should find out (before your first semester if possible) the current grading norms in your new institution. Don't be too tough, and don't become known as an easy grader.

Either reputation hurts you. Award the grades you believe each student earned.

97. KEEP UP WITH TECHNOBABBLE. For many, the latest technical jargon—be it *Twitter, tweet, friending, iPhone, Android, Cliq,* or *Chrome* (especially when some terms also have conventional meanings)—is as impenetrable as the names of hard rock groups are to a devotee of classical music.[6] The terms all sound like technobabble, just as Freudian terms once sounded like psychobabble. Technobabble is what your students know, how they talk, how they write, and how they think. You may even learn words from them that you can use in teaching.

One of us developed a strategy for participating in a conversation with his children and grandchildren about contemporary rock groups. Since all the group names they mention sound as unfamiliar as technical terms, he makes up group names: "Have you heard the latest from Justifiable Homicide?" or "Are you a fan of Speed Bumps?"

98. WIKIPEDIA AND OTHER WEB SOURCES.[7] When you assign students a topic for a paper or ask them to find facts that are new to them, you have to think about Wikipedia and other Web sources. In some faculties, an ever declining number of professors argue that Western civilization will inexorably decline if you allow any use of the Web. Such arguments are futile. Students will use these easily available sources as they sit in front of their computers in the middle of the night to prepare next morning's homework.

What you need to get across to students is that Wikipedia, like other encyclopedias, does not go into the depth you require of your students when researching a topic. Yes, the Wikipedia entries are clear, relevant, organized, contain the basic facts, and provide a broad overview. The entries get students started, but topics explored in sufficient depth and breadth for the typical assignment are few and far between. You can do two things to wean students from relying only on Wikipedia:

- If your students are freshmen or sophomores, few have spent much time in your school's library. Take them there on a field trip and ask the librarians to explain to the students what they can find there, including special collections in your field. Have them do an assignment evaluating Wikipedia in your subject. You could ask them something like, How good is Wikipedia about Topic A?, or Is Wikipedia useless?
- Warn your students that you can catch plagiarism when two or more students copy the same part of a Wikipedia entry. Explain that such copying is plagiarism even if they did not collude.

99. LETTERS OF REFERENCE FOR STUDENTS. The time will come when you are asked to write letters of reference for your students to help them obtain a job or get into graduate school. Requests will come from students you treasure and from students you barely remember or whose name and face you couldn't put together on a bet. A simple "Jane Jones attended my class last spring and received an A minus" won't do. You should personalize as much as you can. Ask for a résumé if the student has one. We sometimes find it useful to ask the student to write a draft we can start from. It is a win-win situation and a teaching moment. The students think about how they want to present themselves, something few students do on their own. Even better, you are saved from composing a complete personalized letter from scratch. You save time, and you write a better letter of reference.

100. THE STUDENT AS CUSTOMER MANTRA. If you talk to faculty in business or economics you hear this mantra repeatedly: the student is the customer. The corollary is industry's view: the customer is king. Using the language of industry, the customer should have control over the product. In educational terms, it implies that the students should be given more say over what is taught, how it is taught, and how students are judged. Students love this viewpoint, but faculty do not.

Yes, tuition is paid by students, parents, and the school's scholarship funds. But that doesn't make students customers in the same sense as shopping at Amazon does. Most students, particularly graduate students, are motivated and intelligent people making an investment to improve their quality of life.

Students commit to their bachelor's, master's, or PhD education in chunks. It is really difficult to switch schools, because credits do not always transfer, requirements differ, and total time to degree increases. In short, once they commit to a school, students are usually stuck until they obtain a degree.

Students do have some influence. For example, over 40 years ago, schools introduced teaching evaluations. Students pushed back by asking for better facilities, fewer Friday classes, and grade inflation (Hint 96). They rarely ask for more intellectual content. When one business administration dean was asked by a student whether he considered him a customer, the dean replied, "Let's get this straight. You may be paying tuition, but the recruiting companies are the customers—you are merely product."

Notes

1. We consider writing this book to be a form of mentoring from a distance. Excellent sources on mentoring include these instructive and highly inspirational books: J. Nakamura and David J. Shernoff, with C. Hooker, *Good Mentoring: Fostering Excellent Practice in Higher Education* (San Francisco, CA: John Wiley, 2009); P. Palmer, *The Courage to Teach* (San Francisco, CA: Jossey-Bass, 2007); J. Parini, *The Art of Teaching* (New

York: Oxford University Press, 2005); S. Strogatz, *The Calculus of Friendship: What a Teacher and a Student Learned About Life While Corresponding About Math* (Princeton, NJ: Princeton University Press, 2009)

2. The ideas in Hints 79, 80, and 111 were inspired by Rob Weir's "10 Commandments of Lecturing," *Inside Higher Ed*, March 20, 2009, http://www.insidehighered.com/advice/instant_mentor/weir3.

3. For more about clickers see D. Buff, *Teaching with Classroom Response Systems: Creative Active Learning Environments* (San Francisco, CA: Jossey-Bass, 2009).

Clickers are hand-held devices similar to TV remotes but with only a few options. The student's electronic response is received by a computer (like your portable) whose software identifies the student and records his or her answer. The software performs simple statistics you can show as bar graphs on a screen at the front of the room. The students can compare their answers to the correct one. In a typical class students use clickers multiple times. Usually the school provides the software, but the student buys the clicker for a nominal sum and uses it in several classes.

4. Sloan Consortium, "Going the Distance: Online Education in the United States, 2011," http://sloanconsortium.org/publications/survey/going_distance_2011.

5. See S. Roistacher and C. Healy, "Grading in American Colleges and Universities," *Teachers College Record*, March 4, 2010.

6. Yes, we know these words will be old hat by the time you read them, but they were new when we wrote this. Substitute your own if you don't like ours.

7. For more about this hint, see R. Weir, "Does Wikipedia Suck?" *Inside Higher Ed*, March 26, 2010, http://www.insidehighered.com/advice/instant_mentor/weir22.

6

RESEARCH

HINT 104: LEARN GRANTSMANSHIP . . . Don't be snobbish!

WHETHER YOU ARE AFFILIATED WITH a research or a teaching institution, you will want to keep up your research. As we said in Hint 70, teaching is a great personal satisfaction, but research productivity is your prime form of portable wealth.

Doing research is a lot easier if you receive a grant from your institution or from an outside source. Unfortunately, most novice faculty have no idea how to obtain grants. Therefore, we include six hints on grantsmanship in this chapter as well as hints about research.

101. IF YOU WANT A RESEARCH CAREER, MAKE SURE THE POSITION YOU ARE OFFERED ALLOWS YOU TO ACTUALLY DO RESEARCH. If at all possible, negotiate in advance with your future department chair and dean about your conditions of work. Ask for reduced teaching loads and committee assignments in your first years, seed money for research expenses until you get your grants, equipment (particularly computing equipment), graduate assistants, and more. In particular, obtain a guarantee that you will teach the same courses for the first few years. Your teaching ratings will be better, and you will not divert your energies from research by preparing new courses. Since many of these requests soak up scarce resources, get them written into your offer letter. If you start without them, it is highly unlikely you will get them later. Even in a tough job market, most of these goodies can be negotiated. Once you are selected, especially if you are the first choice, the department is just as hot for you as you are for it.

102. You can trade off teaching loads and research opportunities. The terms themselves speak volumes about the priorities in many leading universities where, unfortunately, committed and effective teaching is low in status. If you do little research, you will not be tenured in a research (i.e., publish or perish) institution. If you do even a little research in some teaching institutions, it may be held against you; certainly, if you do a lot of research it will not be considered a good thing. You can tell what kind of institution you are dealing with by examining the teaching load. Four or five three-unit classes every semester leave most people so exhausted they do not have the energy to do research on any reasonable time scale. They truly carry a load. In a research institution, faculty typically teach two or three courses a semester and are encouraged to obtain outside funding to support their research activities and to reduce their teaching loads. (Be aware that if you use research funds to reduce teaching time, you will not see a penny of it. The money goes to the institution.) If you intend to do research, seek research opportunities.

103. Research requires quantitative and qualitative skills. Each skill provides different kinds of insights. Be aware that many qualitative researchers consider quantitative types to be mindless empiricists who fail to grasp the subtleties and nuances of the human experience. And many quantitative researchers believe that all true science is quantitative and, furthermore, that qualitative researchers just aren't smart enough to master mathematical techniques. Both of these attitudes are ridiculous.

Regardless of your own research style, master both qualitative and quantitative methods. If you don't, a Neanderthal on the tenure committee could cast a negative vote.

104. Learn grantsmanship. It is a skill like any other. If necessary, attend special workshops. Educate yourself about who funds your type of research. Don't be snobbish! You may feel deep down that you did not train yourself for a life of the mind only to become a peddler of slick prose to federal and foundation bureaucrats. But an ability to raise money can have a seismic effect on your career. Simply imagine yourself as one of two finalists for the plum academic position you always dreamed about. Your competitor has a $600,000 grant and you don't. What are the odds in your favor?

105. DON'T BE MODEST WHEN WRITING A GRANT PROPOSAL. Present the potential contribution of your proposal in the best possible light.

Keep the budget small or at least reasonable. Remember that funding agencies like sure things, not risks. They'll give a little money to an unknown, but for a large amount they'll want one of the powerful 100 (Hint 2) with a track record as a security blanket.

Provide more details than you think necessary about the procedures you will follow. Your friends and colleagues know you are skilled at routine procedures, such as questionnaire surveys or statistical analysis, but a skeptical reviewer who has never heard of you needs to be reassured.

106. PROTEST IF YOUR BRILLIANT GRANT PROPOSAL IS DECLINED. Foundations never use the word *rejected*. Tell the agency that you understand its funds are limited but explain why the research is valuable. It will not change the decision; however, it may pave the way for you to resubmit the idea in the next fiscal year or for you to get favorable treatment on the next one.

If your proposal is declined, ask if you can obtain a copy of the reviews. Of course, this requires a thick skin. But you may learn how you can strengthen the proposal for the next time around.

107. BUILD AN ADVISORY PANEL OF NATIONALLY RESPECTED EXPERTS INTO YOUR GRANT PROPOSAL.[1] Your proposal will be a little more likely to be funded. If it is, you will benefit from the advice of

the experts, and you will expand your network among the top people in the field. Be careful, however. If a national leader agrees to be
listed in three or more of your proposals that are declined, he or she
may conclude you are a loser. Shuffle the panels from proposal to
proposal.

108. IF YOU DIDN'T BUILD IN AN ADVISORY PANEL, IT'S NOT TOO
LATE. If you get the grant, it is not too late to create an advisory
panel to achieve visibility. Once funded, invite some of the leading
people in your field to participate on your advisory panel (Hint 2).
Often you can get them to consult in this way for free or for modest
stipends, certainly much less than their outside consulting fee.

109. GET THE GRANT APPROVAL IN WRITING. Don't count on a
grant or contract until you receive the signed letter of approval.
(Some people say you should wait until you've cashed the first
check.) Some government and foundation officials enthusiastically
encourage ideas they later decline. They will blame the change,
sometimes appropriately, on their external reviewers or on their advisory committee. Remember, things change. Don't believe them
until they sign, even if they guarantee funding for the project.

110. GET CLEARANCE BEFORE YOU STUDY AN ORGANIZATION. If
your research (or that of your students) involves studies of an organization that require interviews with their people, be sure to get
clearance for your work before you start, not after completion. No
matter how trivial a statement may seem to you, administrators of
organizations—private, nonprofit, governmental, or educational—
are extremely sensitive about what is said about them. Their public
relations groups and their army of lawyers see negative publicity
even where no one else does. You risk a lawsuit (and so does your
school) if you proceed without their clearance. Even with clearance

before you start, they may insist on reviewing the results and can come back and say no. Everyone is in the public relations game these days.

Consider the following:

1. If your research is gathered from public sources, you don't need approval, as long as you don't libel the sponsoring organization.
2. Clearance from the sponsor is needed, even if you have institutional review board clearance (Hint 111).

111. INSTITUTIONAL REVIEW BOARDS (IRBs). Your IRB is not the 15th-century Spanish Inquisition, no matter how onerous its name. The IRB performs critical human subject oversight on scientific, ethical, and regulatory issues, particularly for behavioral and biomedical research. IRBs are faculty committees with institution-wide representation that approve, monitor, and review all research involving humans. Their duties and responsibilities are enshrined in the law and in government regulations. You must obtain their approval before you start your work and before you make any changes in your research. They also set time limits on how long their approval is valid. If your research project takes longer than forecast, you must obtain a renewal.

As you plan your research, find out about your local IRB. What do its members look for? What don't they like? The more you know about them before you present your plans the better off you will be.

We recommend you take the nationally respected National Institutes of Health online workshop to learn about IRB issues. It is only 90 minutes long and will answer most of your questions about the IRB and human subjects research. After completing the course and passing a simple test, you receive a certificate and a unique ID number. Many government proposals require you to present this ID number.

112. ACADEMIC TRADE JOURNALS ARE SOURCES OF HIGHER EDUCA-
TION (AND JOB) INFORMATION. Trade journals are published for almost all fields including higher education. The two leading ones are
the *Chronicle of Higher Education* and *Inside Higher Ed.* The *Chronicle* is a weekly that contains more and has a broader range of information but is more traditional than *Inside Higher Ed.* The *Chronicle*
in paper form is expensive, while the much smaller *Inside Higher Ed*
is a free e-journal that shows up in your e-mail every morning. Both
contain job information at no cost to the user. The *Chronicle's* job
information, which is free on the Internet, serves as a publication of
record for equal employment opportunities and hence has the
largest number of listings.[2] *Inside Higher Ed* tends to have a narrower range of jobs.

113. COLLABORATE AND COOPERATE. You are not alone either as a
graduate student or as a young faculty member. You cooperate and
collaborate with many others. Even the dissertation is not a one-
person effort. You work with an adviser and a committee, with the
people you study if your work involves human subjects (Hint 111),
and you interact with fellow graduate students while working on
your topic. When you begin your academic career, you need not sit
off in a corner and try to do it all by yourself. You can collaborate
and cooperate with peers, senior faculty, and even students.

In a research institution, you will collaborate on projects with
coauthors. Most will be close by, but others are from your doctoral
program or people you know through conferences (Hint 193) and
other professional interactions. Your teaching assistants and your
students will help you with specific tasks, including routine ones.
You become part of an ongoing group that cooperates on projects,
reads and critiques each other's papers before submission, gives you
ideas, and receives ideas from you. It is a two-way relationship you
need to cultivate. Although telecommuting (Hint 175) is needed to

obtain integrated blocks of time, you should allocate some time on campus for collaboration and cooperation. It will make you more productive and enrich your life as an academic.

114. PLAGIARISM IS A NO-NO. Plagiarism (Hint 90) is a form of cheating, which may be committed by your students. But you may also wittingly or unwittingly commit plagiarism, particularly in research papers or books. *Plagiarism* is defined by the Institute for Operations Research and the Management Sciences, which publishes many A-list journals, as "copying of ideas, text, data and other creative work (e.g., tables, figures and graphs) and presenting it as your original work without proper citation."[3]

You need to know and observe the following:

- You *cannot* claim the ideas of others as yours, whether or not you express them in the same way as your source.
- If you copy word for word, you must identify the source and you must put the copied material in quotation marks or, if long, in an indented paragraph.
- You can copy from yourself. However, if you signed away the copyright in return for being published, you *must* obtain permission from the copyright holder even though you wrote the book or article yourself. For more on self-plagiarism, see Hint 216.
- The legal limits on how long a quotation can be are relatively vague. If in doubt, get permission. You (or preferably your institution) may have to pay for permission to quote.

115. BACK UP, BACK UP, BACK UP YOUR RESEARCH. Don't be victimized by unexpected electronic failures that could destroy your files. Always back up important electronic files, including your raw data and the draft text of your research.

If you have questionnaires or computer output, keep the originals at least until the dissertation is handed in. After editing or modifying a draft chapter, save it both on your computer and on removable media such as a flash drive. Print out a copy from time to time. Back up text frequently.

Similarly, keep all valuable devices (including computers and removable media) that hold important valuable information secure from theft. Do not assume that theft won't occur in the ivory tower or when you travel (Hint 197). We will spare you the horror stories we have heard.

116. OF THE PEOPLE WHO RECEIVE A PhD, THE MODE FOR THE NUMBER OF PUBLICATIONS IS 0 FOLLOWED CLOSELY BY 1. That is, if you count how many manuscripts people actually publish, you will see that more publish 0 or 1 than any other number. If you publish something while in graduate school, you are much more likely to keep publishing after you finish. If you are a researcher, be thankful for this statistic. It reduces the competition for the limited number of papers a journal can publish in an issue. If you are a teacher, take solace in these modal values because they show that many other people, like you, value the art of teaching over research.

Notes

1. Major think tanks, for example, maintain rosters of such experts, including Nobel Prize winners, who agree to be available for such panels.

2. The link for the *Chronicle*'s jobs page is http://chronicle.com/section/Jobs/61.

3. Institute for Operations Research and the Management Sciences, *INFORMS Guidelines for Plagiarism*, October 21, 2009, http://www.informs.org/content/downloads/file/INFORMS%20Plagiarism%20policy.pdf.

7

TENURE

HINT 126: THE TENURE CLOCK IS REALLY
FOUR AND A HALF YEARS, NOT SEVEN.

THE MOST DREADED EXPERIENCE FOR AN ACADEMIC is the tenure process. Without tenure, you cannot stay permanently at an institution as a professor, and you must go job hunting in an uncertain market. Some schools may consider it a stain on your record if you tried but failed to obtain tenure; with it, you remove uncertainty.

Some large, often unionized, state institutions undertake reviews that reduce the trauma by letting people know where they stand as they go along. Others undertake stringent three-year reviews in which some are fired and others are given warnings and firm instructions on what they should do over the next three years to gain tenure. However, because administrators and criteria can change, these reviews do not guarantee tenure will be granted.

117. TENURE IS THE PRIZE. Although things are changing, it is still true that tenure is the goal in academia. Many non-tenure-track jobs are exciting in higher education and in research organizations, but most new PhDs seeking academic careers want to become tenured professors.

118. YOUR PROMOTION DOSSIER. When you are reviewed for tenure or promotion, the review committee members use a dossier about your work, usually prepared by the committee chair. At most institutions, you prepare the first draft of that dossier. What an opportunity! Review committees and committee chairs are often lazy. They probably will not edit your text heavily. For example, if you say, "Professor Jones is the most productive, creative sociologist in the last 50 years," they might leave this sentence in the final draft.

Typical dossiers consist of

- an introduction, including the review process;
- a brief description of your career before appointment, your education, and prior employment;
- your research program if you work at a research university;
- a detailed description of your publications (with copies of publications enclosed);
- your approach to teaching and your teaching reviews;
- comments from student letters solicited for the review, which are signed at some institutions by students, although their names and identifying text are removed to protect confidentiality; and
- your service to the school and/or the community.

Your chair obtains the outside reviewers and student letters, and describes the review process. You prepare the rest.

Preparing a dossier is an onerous chore. Some items, like teaching evaluations and even copies of your publications, may be difficult to find. We recommend you begin setting up a dossier the week you begin the position and accumulate elements for it as they become available.

119. WHY TENURE IS SUCH A HURDLE. Consider the cost of a positive tenure decision to your institution. Assume you are making $66,666 when you come up for tenure and will serve the university 30 years after tenure. Further, assume your academic raises cover only the cost of living (the worst case from your point of view, the best from the university's); that is, your salary is nearly the same in real terms for the rest of your career. From your point of view, you certainly think of yourself as worth the $2 million bet the university must make. But think of it from the university's viewpoint. If it awards tenure when it shouldn't, the school made a bad $2 million bet. If it denies tenure to someone and that person many years later wins a Nobel Prize, everyone will conclude, "Old Siwash University was stupid." However, that buzz will last only for a few days, and the affair will blow over. Although it will cost the school something to hire your replacement if you are denied tenure, with any luck your replacement will work for even less than you did. Any statistician will tell you that given these upside and downside risks, universities are absolutely rational to err on the *no* side, not on the *yes* side.

120. IF BY CHANCE YOU ACHIEVE TENURE, NEVER TAKE ANOTHER APPOINTMENT WITHOUT IT. The people who promise tenure "real soon" may not be there when the crunch comes. See Hint 1.

121. TENURE, LIKE RESEARCH SUPPORT (Hint 64), CAN BE NEGOTIATED ON THE WAY IN. Nobody tells you (and nobody admits it), but tenure is, in effect, transferable. Be firm in your position that you wouldn't think of moving without being tenured at the new institution.

122. TENURE IS TOUGHER TO OBTAIN IN CROSS-DISCIPLINARY FIELDS. You are judged by the standards of people who made their mark in a single, well-established discipline. For example, information systems, which is taught in business schools, combines a hard science (computer science) and two soft sciences (organizational behavior and management). People in this field publish at the intersection of disciplines. However, they are judged by people in the pure disciplines and are expected to contribute to these pure disciplines. Research that combines existing ideas from several disciplines is discounted by purists even though it is the essence of the field.

123. TENURE IS FOREVER (ALMOST). When you retire, forever ends. There is a roughly 50% chance you will be involved with your tenured colleagues longer than you will be connected to your spouse or partner.

We know of only three exceptions to this professional lifetime commitment. Inasmuch as they happen rarely, we don't think you should lose sleep over them.

- If the university closes your department, technically it has the right to dismiss the professors in that department. Even then, however, administrators can choose instead to reassign professors to other departments or help them find another position. Remember too (Hint 121), if you move to another school, tenure is usually transferable.
- You can be fired if the university claims moral turpitude. These offenses can take the form of a felony, theft from the university, plagiarism, and more. If university administrators really want to fire you, they look for alleged moral turpitude that could make headlines in the *National Enquirer* so they are not on the hook if you fight back.
- The five-year reviews instituted by many institutions allow schools to fire you if you do not produce up to standard as determined by a faculty committee. (See Hint 132)

124. TENURE AS WE KNOW IT TODAY MAY NOT BE HERE FOREVER. The problem stems from changes in the retirement law and in public attitudes. Since 1992, by law you cannot be forced to retire once you reach some arbitrary retirement age. Thus, universities that grant tenure are stuck with you as long as you want to work, whether you perform or not. The teaching life is fulfilling, and the paycheck is better than your retirement income.[1] Besides, what would you do with yourself in retirement? When our colleague, the late Peter Drucker (who was still teaching full-time at age 92), was asked why he didn't retire, he replied, "Why retire at 65? I can't see myself driving a Winnebago for 25 years."

125. THE NUMBER OF TENURED SLOTS MAY DECREASE WITH TIME. In their 2006 book on the American professoriate, Jack Schuster and Martin Finkelstein report data that show that the number of part-time and full-time hires who are off the tenure track increased significantly, from a few percent in the late 1970s to over 50% today.[2] It is not clear whether this change is the result of universities' hedging their bets because they fear enrollments will go down in some areas, whether it is a deliberate move to reduce the size (and with it, the power) of the tenured faculty, or whether they simply want to reduce their payroll.

The Mechanics of Tenure

126. THE TENURE CLOCK IS REALLY FOUR AND A HALF YEARS, NOT SEVEN. Remember, the rule is that the seventh contracted year is forever. Thus, the latest the tenure decision can be made is in year six. Your dossier must be completed for the powers that be by the beginning of year six. Although you can count publications that are accepted, journal (or book manuscript) review time averages more than a year in most fields. Therefore you need to submit your work for publication by the beginning of year five. It will take you six months to write your results. Ergo, four and a half years.

127. THE DREADED IMPACT FACTOR. Not only are schools ranked (Hint 44) from highest to lowest,[3] but so are academic journals. The Institute for Scientific Information in Philadelphia created a measure it calls the *impact factor*, a numerical measure of prestige for each journal. For a given journal, it is based on the ratio of A/B where

- A = number of times articles published in year i and $i + 1$ were cited by indexed journals in year $i + 2$ (e.g., articles published in 2009 and 2010 cited in 2011)
- B = total number of citable items in that journal in years i and $i + 1$
- The ratings for year $i + 2$ are published in year $i + 3$

Although the system may seem unfair and a poor approximation for long-term impact, the numbers produced are considered holy.[4] The ratings are published with fanfare by journals that receive high rankings.

Worse, many tenure and promotion committees use these numbers to judge whether your work is important. Fortunately, not all your publications have to be in top-ranked journals. Tenure committees usually also look for bulk, that is, how many publications you authored. You are allowed to (and should) find journals to publish your less valuable articles (i.e., stinkers) to obtain bulk (Hint 1 and Hint 4).

128. TENURE COMMITTEES LOOK ALMOST EXCLUSIVELY AT REFEREED PUBLICATIONS that appear in peer-reviewed journals or in scholarly books. It is, in a sense, a tragedy that you get much more credit for what appears in a *write only* journal (i.e., a journal with a minute circulation) than for what appears in a high-circulation, widely read popular magazine. But that is the way the game is played.

129. DOWNLOAD COUNTS. Members of tenure and review committees like candidates who develop a personal reputation thus reflecting glory on the institution. Impact factors (Hint 127) are one crude measure. Another is the download count. If you have an academic publication that is accessible on the Internet, is anybody reading it, or better yet, downloading it? Some publishers maintain download counts and send them to authors. If you are fortunate to receive download counts, keep them. They are handy at tenure and performance review time.

130. MULTIPLE-AUTHOR PAPERS. In Hints 232 and 233 in Chapter 13 we advise you to make sure you are the sole author of some of your publications and tell you of the risks of being a coauthor with superstars. We do not mean to imply that being a coauthor is always risky or dangerous. It is not. Working with people you know, even if they are at another institution far away, can be exhilarating because of the spark of ideas as you play off one another. In some fields (e.g., chemistry and medicine) lengthy author lists are the norm, particularly if a project is large.

Early in a research project, you and your coauthors need to discuss candidly the order in which the names will appear on the publication. Have this discussion long before the article is about to be submitted.

131. PUBLICATION QUALITY COUNTS. While we think academic priorities should be different, in real life tenure committees focus almost exclusively on publications in peer-reviewed journals (Hint 128), the higher they are ranked (Hint 44), and the more impact (Hint 127) they have, the better.[5] Of course, the quantity of your publications is also critical (Hint 1).

Value quality highly. Try to make each article you submit to a journal about a single topic of importance. Conduct your research with a solid, rigorous design. Write as clearly as possible. Try to produce each article as though it were the one example of your work that will be remembered.

132. ROLLING REVIEWS. The university's objective is different from yours. They want to avoid deadwood, and they take age as prima facie evidence of your being past it. They certainly want you out of there before Alzheimer's disease impedes your performance. If the number of positions is constricted, the administration would prefer to take your slot and give it to a bright young person who is more current, may work for less, and who revitalizes your department. Tenure forces a university to hold on to you because firing you because of your age would be discrimination. Younger faculty who want new opportunities generally side with the university. As a result, some universities have introduced a *rolling* tenure arrangement in which tenured full (and sometimes associate) professors are reviewed every five years and may be encouraged to leave because of poor performance.

The mechanics of the eternal five-year rolling review, while usually not as rigorous as tenure itself, look at what you've accomplished. Such tangibles as teaching evaluations and research publication records are examined by a special faculty committee, often constituted uniquely for each professor. Penalties for poor performance can range from recommendations for improvement in the next five-year interval to a recommendation that you be fired. The latter option is extremely rare, but not unheard of. Most institutions allow several opportunities for improvement. Don't assume tenure protects you against negative five-year reviews.

Our indications are that rolling reviews result in making senior people work a little harder. They became professors because they are risk averse and therefore want to avoid consequences. The best protection against a negative review is to produce as a teacher, as a scholar, and as a citizen of your institution.

We recommend you keep your résumé up to date and maintain records of what you accomplished from the day you started at your institution. It will make your reviews easier. Furthermore, if the verdict is negative, you've at least generated material needed to obtain your next appointment.

Notes

1. It gets even better if you reach 70 1/2, because you can then take money out of your tax-deferred retirement nest egg and still collect your paycheck as well as your Social Security benefits.

2. J. H. Schuster and M. J. Finkelstein, *The American Faculty: The Restructuring of Academic Work and Careers* (Baltimore, MD: Johns Hopkins University Press, 2006).

3. Rankings and even citation counts are suspect numbers (e.g., Hint 129).

4. For example, one of Einstein's major works is the one most cited, but would have barely been noticed in the number of citations in the two years following publication.

5. See note 3 above.

8

ACADEMIC RANK

HINT 134: AS A FULL PROFESSOR, YOU MUST BE KNOWN FOR SOMETHING.

JUST LIKE GRADE INFLATION, RANK INFLATION is a sign of our times. It used to be that people with new PhDs were hired as instructors and then rose to assistant, associate, and full professor. Today, only the last three of these remain. Tenure usually is the transition to associate. Full professor is, of course, the desired state.

133. BEING A TENURED FULL PROFESSOR IS AS CLOSE TO FREEDOM AS YOU CAN COME in U.S. society. Yes, you must meet your classes. However, when you walk into your office in the morning, it is you who decides what you should be working on, not someone else. You can decide to continue what you have been working on or delve into something new. You are limited only by your imagination. It is a state much desired by others and one you achieved.

134. AS A FULL PROFESSOR, YOU MUST BE KNOWN FOR SOMETHING. When you reach the exalted state of tenured associate professor, the time has come to see the big picture and undertake large, long-term research projects so you can become a full professor. Unfortunately, you spent the previous six years (and your dissertation time) doing small, short-term research projects, each designed to earn you a publication or two so you could achieve tenure. You were never taught how to conduct a large project. As a result, you are back in a learning situation. Merely doing more of what you did as an assistant professor doesn't cut it in major institutions because the promotion committees ask different questions. Having survived the tenure process, everyone knows you can do research. But to be a full professor, you must be known for something.

135. AVOID BECOMING THE PITIED PERMANENT ASSOCIATE PRO-
FESSOR. It is a dead end. You are given all the committee assignments no one else wants. Although people are nice to Permanent
Associate Professors, behind their back they cluck about "poor
Smith." It is important for you to remember that if you stay an
associate professor for too long, the time for promotion passes
you by. This interval varies from institution to institution. However, while you are still an assistant, it will pay you to gauge how
long it usually takes people in your school or department to be
promoted. Try to be in the middle, or earlier, of the promotion
time distribution. Remember too that you must have done something to merit promotion.

136. PROMOTION IS A UNIQUE OPPORTUNITY FOR A LARGER PAY
RAISE. When you are promoted to associate professor, or from associate to full professor, you have a unique opportunity to request a
substantial pay increase. As implied in Hint 33, most universities
provide minimal raises for faculty each year; however, many make
exceptions for a promotion.

9

YOUR FINANCIAL
LIFE AS AN
ACADEMIC

HINT 144: ADMINISTRATORS MAKE MORE than professors . . . to cope with the stress that comes from the many nasty things they need to do.

YOU SHOULD NEGOTIATE for the highest initial salary possible, because as we indicated in Hint 33, except for promotion or tenure, you are tied to the average annual raise the institution gives. This section discusses some of the factors you need to understand as well as the ins and outs of working now on funding your retirement nest egg. Income from sources outside the university are discussed in Appendix B.

137. ACADEMICS ARE RISK AVERSE. We grant that exceptions exist, but most people going into university teaching are risk averse. They seek security. To them, a dollar at age 70 is as important (or nearly so) as a dollar at age 30. They are willing to take a lower-paying job at 30, because with tenure they can expect not to be thrown out on the street at age 50, as happens in other employment sectors, with no possibility of finding another job when a reduction in head count takes place. That is, academics have a low discount rate for the future.

138. CONTRACTS ARE GIVEN TO FACULTY FOR NINE MONTHS.[1] The other three months are supposedly for you to do with as you please. For example, if you receive, say, $54,000 a year, you are being paid $6,000 a month while working. However, the institution usually pays you in 12 installments, so your monthly check is $4,500 before deductions.

139. SALARIES VARY BY FIELD. Philosophers make less than business school professors, who make less than law school faculty, all of whom make less than physicians teaching in medical schools. For some reason, people in mathematics do well. Exceptions occur in some institutions (typically in state and community colleges) where salary is determined by rank (and step in rank). It doesn't matter whether your specialty is hospitality or nuclear physics.

140. SUMMER PAY. The three months' "vacation" you receive can, in theory, be spent by you in any way you please. Go to the seashore or abroad, write a book, or work on papers needed for tenure. In practice, young faculty work during the summer for money to supplement the low salaries they accepted (see Hint 63). Teaching summer school, if offered to you, is usually paid miserably.

141. THE ZERO RAISE YEARS. Faculty members generally receive a raise in their contract letter for the following year. If you talk with the faculty at conferences or in your own school, they may recall one or more years in which the amount of the raise was zero for everyone, usually because the institutions or legislatures encountered financial difficulty. Because next year's raise tends to be a percentage of this year's salary, a zero raise is rarely recovered in future years.

142. RETIREMENT SAVINGS. For graduate students and newly minted PhDs, retirement seems like an irrelevant, distant abstraction. It shouldn't be. You should plan for your retirement when you take your first full-time academic job. In Hint 61 we advised you to inquire about the retirement plan before you accept an appointment and told you about the two major systems (TIAA–CREF and state plans) in the United States. In this hint, we offer more information about your retirement options.[2]

Of course, some faculty members choose not to retire. Our late colleague Peter Drucker was a prime example. Well into his 90s, he continued to teach, consult, and write major books. He never retired from professional activities or the university. He was an exception.

Most professors (including you) do retire at some age. Years ago that age was a mandatory 65. Today, typical professors teach at least until they are 70. At whatever age you retire, you need to consider your retirement finances.

The absolute base is your Social Security income. You and your employer contribute to Social Security as long as you are employed, unless you work in an exempt state system. Unfortunately, Social Security income will be well below your ending salary.

Most retirement plans involve payroll deductions made by you and contributions by the institution. University plans fall under Section 403(b) of the tax code rather than 401(k) used by industry. The plans are different for state and private institutions. Some institutions provide you with a choice among multiple plans, but most don't. Retirement money is usually tax sheltered. That is, you don't pay tax on any contribution or its growth until you draw it out after retirement.

Diversify your investments. Don't put all your money into high-growth stocks that pay off big when the stock market goes up but collapse in an instant if the market tanks, as it did in fall 2008. You could lose a lot of what you put aside. In the same vein, don't put all your funds in slow-growth but safe blue chip investments, bonds, or bank savings accounts. While they are safer and hedge against dips in the market, you miss the growth and profits in a rising bull market.

Retirement is a consideration when you start your first appointment and when you change schools. If you go from one TIAA–CREF institution to another, the plans are almost identical, although the amount of the contributions by the institutions may differ. Going from TIAA–CREF to a state system means a different set of rules. The amount you receive from a state system may depend on the number of years of service and the three highest-earning years. Knowing whether you can roll over your account from your present plan to the new one becomes an important factor in evaluating the real income you receive.

Money invested in retirement at a young age yields much more than the same amount invested 20 years later. Study the compound interest curve. Essentially the value of your retirement nest egg grows slowly initially. However, because neither what you and your school put in nor the interest is taxed, your principal skyrockets in later years.

Don't retire early. The longer you stay employed and supported by your regular pay, the more your retirement nest egg grows. And more important, the greater your annuity. Annuities are based on the number of years of life expectancy from the date of retirement. Assume you're expected to live until 90. Put simply, retiring at 65 leaves you with a smaller nest egg that must be spread over a life expectancy of 25 years, rather than a larger nest egg if you retire at 75 that will be spread over 15 years.

Note: As we write this hint in 2011, Congress and state legislatures are trying to tinker with retirement promises and the interest rate is nearing zero. Social Security and annuities are in danger of being changed negatively for young faculty. Be sure to follow closely the debates and the actions taken.

If you are wise and save now, you will thank us for this advice in 40 years.

143. TAX DEFERRAL. If you can afford it (and unfortunately many young professors cannot) or you receive extra funds such as from consulting or inheritances, put some of the money away as savings for retirement. Various retirement accounts, such as IRAs, simplified employee pension plans (SEPs), and supplemental retirement annuities (SRAs), are available on a tax-deferred basis.[3] If possible, contribute each month to such a plan. The benefits accrued years from now are enormous.

The key point is that your savings are tax deferred, meaning you don't pay taxes now on the amount you save. For example, if you put away $300 per month it only costs you $200 per month.[4] That is, if you didn't invest that $300, you would only see $200 more in your take-home pay. Furthermore, the interest accumulates and your money increases even further. Of course, you eventually must pay the taxes when you retire, but usually it is at a reduced tax rate if your retirement income is lower than your present income.

144. ADMINISTRATORS MAKE MORE. Administrators usually are paid more than professors. Admittedly, most administrators were once professors who abandoned that calling. They usually also ask for extra pay to cope with the stress that comes from the many nasty things they need to do. Because they work for the entire year, their pay is based on 12 months. A $54,000 academic salary becomes $72,000 even before a bonus for administration. And, oh yes, they usually receive one month of vacation.

However, administrators—be they presidents, deans, or functionaries—are not tenured as administrators. Therefore they must make their money now because they can (and generally will) be out on the street (or return to teaching) if they make a misstep or become unpopular. For example, the optimistic estimate for the half life of a dean of a business school is five years. As the present focus on accountability increases, administrator half lives decrease (implying that risks increase). Hence, they seek financial incentives to accept the increased risk.

Notes

1. In some schools, the contract is for 10 months.

2. In many schools, particularly private ones, retirement packages for senior faculty are often negotiated privately. Check with recent retirees to find out if such negotiations are available at your school.

3. An alphabet soup of tax deferred plans are available through TIAA–CREF, your local bank, and mutual funds. Educational funds provide annuities for your children's college tuition. The names and the terms of plans available change over time depending on congressional legislation.

4. The numbers shown assume your federal and state income taxes equal roughly one third of your net income. Your individual circumstances may vary.

10

LIFE AS AN ACADEMIC

HINT 185: NEVER, EVER BECOME A DEPARTMENT CHAIR . . . unless you're a tenured full professor.

NOW THAT YOU KNOW ABOUT FINDING A JOB, the things you need to do to reach full professor, and the financial aspects of academia, we turn to the things that affect your day-to-day life. This chapter, and the subsections, such as being an institutional citizen, becoming a department chair, and dealing with grievances, should help you understand the life you are preparing to undertake.

145. GOOD DEANS/BAD DEANS. Good deans try to make your life better. They help your school and department (and you) increase their reputation. They help in obtaining resources, grants, and chaired positions. Bad deans can make your life miserable. Don't assume that because the half life of deans is five years (Hint 144), you can outlast them. Get out your résumé.

146. NEVER, EVER CHOOSE SIDES IN DEPARTMENT POLITICS. The side you are on expects your support because its members know they are right. They will give you no reward for it. The side you are not on will remember forever.

147. DON'T ACCEPT A JOINT APPOINTMENT, particularly as your initial appointment. The chairperson of each department will assume the other chairperson will take care of you. Each department chair will assume he or she owns at least three fourths of you. Furthermore, at raise, promotion, and tenure times, each department will judge you only on the papers you published in its own discipline.

148. JOIN THE FACULTY CLUB if your school has one. You will usually be taken there at some time during the interview process. If it is at all typical, it will seem like a cross between your undergraduate dining hall and the stuffy clubs you see on BBC mysteries. If you look around, it may look like a haven for the superannuated.

Don't be deceived. The faculty club can be one of your most important assets. It is a place where you can meet with colleagues without interruptions by smart phones or students. People always feel better when they eat and will often tell you things they would not otherwise reveal. In other words, it is a good place to keep up with what is going on. Being seen there by the older faculty in your department can be a plus because it shows you want to fit in. You will be surprised to find you can actually have occasional intellectual discussions with people from other disciplines. It is also a good place to impress visitors and students. The food, of course, will rapidly become tedious.

149. Office hours are sacred at some institutions. You *must* be in your office at the times you promise. In other schools, they are merely advisory. Know what the situation is at your institution and follow the local custom. In general, you are required to provide certain times for students when they can contact you. Making appointments is one way to do this. If you do make an appointment, be sure to keep it. A reputation for not keeping appointments is as bad as a reputation for not replying to e-mails.

150. Sabbaticals. The best fringe benefit a professor receives is the sabbatical. It is not, repeat not, a vacation. Here are some things you should do on your sabbatical:

1. Do productive work.
2. Use the time for reflection and getting into new things.
3. If at all feasible, leave town and never show your face at the institution during the sabbatical. If you appear, you will be put to work.

4. Stay in touch with your dissertation students. You can meet with them by e-mail or off campus.

5. When your sabbatical is over, write a good report on what you did so the administration will give you another one the next time you are eligible.

Always apply for a sabbatical as soon as you are eligible. Most institutions do not allow you to accumulate the time for future use. If you wait an extra semester or two, you likely will never get the accumulated time back.

151. MAINTAIN COLLEGIALITY. *Collegiality* is a difficult term to define. It involves maintaining good social relations with the people in your department and in related departments around campus. If everyone in your department has coffee in the lounge at 10:00 each morning, be there if you can—even if you only drink mineral water. If colleagues ask you to cover a class or review a draft of their latest paper or serve on a doctoral committee they chair, do it. The web of obligations is two-sided and you will receive reciprocal favors over time. Collegiality is one case where the commitments, even though they take away from your research time, yield positive results. Don't be perceived as a loner or a misanthrope, particularly by senior faculty.

152. AS AN ACADEMIC, YOU ARE A PUBLIC PERSON. Your students spend 40 hours or more a semester doing nothing but looking at you while you talk. This experience makes an indelible impression on them. You will find several years later when they approach you and call you by name, they will expect you to remember them. You, of course, usually will not. Their appearance and dress will be different. The important point is that your behavior in public places is noticed when you least expect it.

153. FREEDOM OF SPEECH. We firmly believe that people should be free to express their views on public issues, whether the views are mainstream or not. But understand the associated career risks. The conventional wisdom that academics are free to say what they please may well be the reason why you chose your career. However, our observation of what really goes on leads us to a different take for untenured faculty. No matter what your position on an issue—popular or unpopular, for or against the environment, for or against gun control—once it becomes known, people on the other side of that issue will inevitably surface. They will consider your position a form of bad judgment and they will hold it against you. Remember that people in academia have long memories. Even if everyone in the department publicly espouses the same cause, you cannot be certain what position each one takes privately. Consider something as seemingly safe as excoriating the oil company that caused the latest oil spill. Your colleagues could be the people who consult with that company, who are writing its corporate history, who have a nephew who works for the company, or who own 3,000 shares of the company's stock. Of course, once you achieve the tenured full professor rank, the situation changes.

154. ATTEND INVITED LECTURES. When world-class people are invited to lecture at your school, even if they are not in your field, be sure to attend if at all possible (and definitely if they are among the 100 powerful people in your field as discussed in Hint 2). When you were in graduate school, intellectually important people would come to campus to give seminars and spend a day or two with faculty and students. Often, these were memorable events in your life. You would attend just to see who these people were. Now that you are a faculty member, don't feel too busy to attend such sessions. Even if the topic doesn't seem interesting to you, go. What you will hear, if you listen carefully, is how they think about the world, how they approach problems, and how they work on them. Often they will change your perspectives in your own areas of teaching and research.

If you are at a small school, you can help bring people to campus to lecture. For example, many professional societies maintain visiting lecturer programs in which people volunteer to visit campuses. Look at the lists and arrange for your department to invite some of them. If you live in a metropolitan area that includes other institutions, get on their mailing list and find out who is coming to visit there. Advertised lectures are open to the public. If you belong to a local chapter of your professional society, work with the program committee to bring interesting people to its meetings.

Remember, lectures are a way to keep up with your field at almost no cost.

155. SERVING AS AN EXTERNAL REVIEWER. As you advance in your career, someone at another college or university will ask you to write an external review for a person up for tenure or promotion. The first time you receive one of these requests you will probably be flattered and think it a high honor to be considered sufficiently knowledgeable or important to undertake the task. Unfortunately, it is not an honor but a ritual schools go through because faculty don't believe what they see in front of their eyes. They've lived with the candidate for five or more years. Yet for tenure and promotions, they ask for evaluations from people who at best met the candidate briefly once at a national meeting.

Why do they do it? On one level, they are celebrity hunters, little different from paparazzi. The more well-known the evaluator, the better. On another level, they do it because that is the way it was always done, and it might, just might, tell them something damaging they did not know before. Better to be safe than sorry.

Some schools allow the candidate to supply a list of people who should be consulted, some (but not all) of whom will be chosen. That's supposed to make it fairer. The wise candidate includes only personal friends in such a list. Such evaluations are window dressing because they only yield letters of praise and contain no real information.

The key question often asked of the evaluator—would you grant tenure to (or promote) this individual at your institution?—dodges the issue, because what is important at your institution is not what is important at the requesting institution.

Evaluations are considered a free good. Deans and committee members don't value the work that goes into the recommendation because they don't pay for it. Yet hundreds of dollars are spent by your school for your own time and that of the secretaries involved. The requesting institution often doesn't even write a thank-you letter, much less let you know the outcome. Your own institution gives you no credit for such work because it is work done for somebody else.

Unless you are well established or the request is completely outside your field, you can't really avoid the task. Usually it includes reviewing attached papers and books (you may not be interested in) and writing an evaluation that answers a set of questions. Fortunately, the amount to be written is not extreme. Our experience is that letters of under one page and much over two pages are considered negatively (you're hiding something significant by saying too little or too much). You should be careful even in a two-page letter. If you think the candidate deserves promotion or tenure, be sure not to write an account that discusses positives *and* negatives. A hint of something negative can be seized upon by a committee member or administrator who is opposed as a reason for saying no. Evaluation letters don't change the politics of the situation.

156. KEEPING UP WITH YOUR FIELD. In every field, things change. You can't keep teaching the same material year in, year out. As a faculty member, you are committed to lifelong learning. Your need for new knowledge doesn't end with your PhD. You need to keep up with the latest developments in your discipline: new theories, models, research findings, and analytic techniques. Here are some strategies:

- Attend conferences (Hint 193) where new ideas are first presented.
- Read the cutting-edge journals and books.
- Use software options, for example, RSS feeds and Google Alerts, to keep abreast of new discoveries.
- Use a research assistant, if you have one, to find and organize new knowledge for you.
- Make new knowledge areas of interest to you the subject for term papers in graduate seminars you teach.

157. YOU CAN GO HOME AGAIN—RETREAT RIGHTS. When you accept a new job—either internal or external to your institution—you may have *retreat rights.* That is, under some circumstances you can go back to the position you held previously. The most visible are people who leave academia to take major government jobs such as the president's economic adviser. Retreat rights also hold for administrators (e.g., department chairs, deans, provosts, and presidents) who typically go back to being a member of the faculty. The policy also applies to research projects, pregnancy, and other situations. Typically, academic institutions let you take a leave of absence of up to two years but will not extend it beyond that time.

158. THE BOARD OF TRUSTEES. You can work an entire career without ever meeting a trustee or thinking about the board. This state of affairs is unfortunate because boards of trustees not only wield enormous power over your institution, they can help you and your department.

If you work at a state university, the board most likely was appointed by the governor. In private institutions, board policies, including the appointment of new trustees, parallel those of other nonprofit organizations. The president of the institution, or a current board member, proposes a new board member; that person is interviewed; and the full board votes to invite him or her to join.

Boards of trustees, for example, provide the ultimate vote on whether you receive tenure (almost always pro forma if recommended by the faculty and the administration), provide the monetary pool available for pay increases (typically a percentage of current expenditures), and decide whether and how the university is reorganized.

In most institutions, the board tends to be more politically conservative than the faculty. After all, one of the board members' major functions is to donate money to the institution. They themselves tend to be wealthy, successful people.

In many institutions, faculty are offered opportunities to meet and talk with board members, for example, during receptions, dinners, and retreats. Some boards even have a faculty and/or a student member. Other boards have the unfortunate tradition of keeping the two groups separate. If you are invited to a board event, attend! Try to get to know one or two board members. They can help you. They may be able to bring visibility to your research or teaching innovations. In fact, they sometimes introduce you to people and organizations that can fund your work.

Your Administrative Life

Even though you are a lone professor, you have an administrative life. For example, you supervise many people even though they don't work for you, and you interact with administrative people.

159. SECRETARIES (now often called *administrative assistants*) ARE A SCARCE RESOURCE. You should treat them as such. Most universities pay secretaries below market wages and expect them to gain psychic income from the academic environment. They often work in physical spaces you would not accept even as a graduate student. (We estimate that the chance of a secretary working in an office with a window is about one in three.) By any standard, they are an exploited class. If you develop a good relationship with them, they will work miracles for you. They know every arcane administrative procedure needed to get things done. They can say nice things about you to people who matter in the department. Remember, however, that if they don't like you, they can kill your reputation.

160. VALUE YOUR TEACHING ASSISTANTS AND GRADERS. After years of being one, you know that research assistants and graders are perceived as the sherpas of academe. Their role is to be as inconspicuous as possible and carry the burdens as their professors climb the mountain of knowledge. It is unfortunately true that many young professors rapidly adopt the same attitude. Doing so is a huge mistake.

161. GRADING. Your students learn from the feedback they receive, and graded papers are an important feedback tool. Thus, you need to pay attention to which answers are considered correct and what criteria are used for grading. In the case of examinations, you should grade papers personally rather than delegating the job to a teaching assistant, if you are assigned one. The examination is a form of communication, of feedback, between the student and you. You find out what the students really know and what principles and concepts did not get through to them.

162. YOUR RESEARCH ASSISTANTS REQUIRE SUPERVISION. Having them take data for your key experiment or survey instrument is appropriate, but the final responsibility for their output is yours. You need to know what they are doing and how well they are doing it. Treat them with respect and show them they are valued. One way to do this is to be generous in sharing authorship with them when they make contributions to your research. In short, you must teach them the art of research. Remember that disgruntled graders or research assistants need not get mad at you; they can easily get even.

163. PHYSICAL PLANT. Like the computer center and other service operations, you must deal with the physical plant department. The people in physical plant are the ones who provide the services you take for granted: moving furniture or fixing heating or changing lightbulbs. Your first contact will typically come when you move into your office.

Many people in physical plant are highly skilled craftspeople who can do wondrous mechanical and electrical things. They know about things you never learned. The physical plant staff works on many jobs simultaneously. Although your problem is the one you think is the most important, it is only one job of many, some of which are emergencies. Physical plant charges for its services. Often it needs to charge quite a lot because the job is much more complex than you realize. Be sure you have a big departmental budget available before you call physical plant.

164. BE CAREFUL WHAT YOU DELEGATE. As a professor you often delegate work to others, be they teaching assistants, department secretaries, or work/study students. Be careful about what you assign and be clear in your instructions. Think of yourself as a supervisor or manager in these situations, which you really are. You will be held responsible for the outcome if they make a mistake. Check their output to make certain it is right. If an error occurs, you will be associated with it, and it will be remembered at the wrong time.

Keep in mind that at times the student's or teaching assistant's course work may be of higher priority to him or her than your assignment, particularly during exam times. You will also find that not all assistants are alike; some need everything defined in detail, others can be given more flexibility.

165. BUSINESS CARDS. When you start out, you want people to remember you and to contact you. It is part of building your image, receiving invitations to participate, and eventually becoming one of the 100 powerful people (Hint 2). Business cards help you achieve these goals. Some departments provide them even to graduate students, particularly if you teach, as part of your financial support. If not, they are an inexpensive and potentially valuable investment, sometimes as little as $10 or $15. In addition to business cards, use your e-mail program to create a signature block that appears with every message you send.

Business cards and signature blocks should contain your name, affiliation, and how to reach you via e-mail, Twitter, snail mail, or other accounts. Always carry business cards with you. You will use them when job hunting, at conferences, when contacting people about fieldwork, dealing with publishers' representatives, and with students.

Your Digital Life

Although some of your more ancient colleagues still resist the personal computer after more than 30 years, you will be immersed in all things digital. This section discusses many ways the digital world changes your academic job. You will already know much of what you find in this section; however, we believe some of the hints that follow will be new and useful. Pick and choose among them.

166. LEARN THE IDIOSYNCRASIES OF YOUR INSTITUTION'S COM-
PUTER CENTER. The probability of your having to deal with the computer center is high, even if you are in the humanities. Although a
computer center is a service organization, it is sometimes staffed by
people who are not service-oriented. This attitude is particularly
true of computer center directors. Treasure the director who is
service-oriented. If your center is not service-oriented, your frustra-
tion level will be high every time you approach the center. Some
directors are super security-conscious. Like the librarian who believes that the best place for a book is on the shelf, such directors
want to keep you from actually using the center because you might
not follow their arbitrary rules.

167. BE REALISTIC ABOUT WHAT YOUR COMPUTER CAN DO FOR YOU.
As an academic, you have great computer availability and great support from the techies among your students. Get to know your computer center people and their abilities.[1] Also learn which research
software is available for free at the center and which needs to be
funded by you or your research grant. Since universities pay all staff
people poorly, you may not have the brightest computerniks working there. Over time you will find the computer people you really
need to consult regularly, just as you find a hairdresser or an auto
mechanic.

We can tell you very little new about how to use computers or
about their idiosyncrasies. Almost everyone who reads this book
will have lived with computers since they could first touch a key-
board. Some warnings:

▪ The personal computer (and the smart phone and the tablet
   computer) can be highly addictive. While providing a wealth of
   information at no or minimal cost, searches can eat up time if
   you are addicted.

- Computers are not secure. Your privacy can be easily invaded. Almost every campus has students with hacking skills who can get into your computer, do malicious things to it, and steal everything from bank account entries to tomorrow's test questions. Be wary.
- Students expect you to be computer savvy in managing your computer and knowing the latest gizmos.
- Over time, expect the computer to be ever more useful in teaching and ever more distracting.

168. THE DOWNSIDE OF E-MAIL. First you must deal with spam, viruses, and spyware. Spam is mail that tries to entice you to spend money for things you don't need. Viruses are *malware* that try to damage your computer or hijack its use for another's gain. Spyware comes in a variety of guises, such as tracking your actions on the computer in the hope of learning about you. As we write, spam is increasing, and its practitioners are becoming more sophisticated about avoiding interdiction. For example, you will be offered great wealth from Nigeria if only you put up a substantial amount of "earnest money."

People will try to get you to open attachments that contain viruses or ask you to provide personal information, such as your credit card, Social Security number, or bank account numbers and passwords, so they can rob you. Know that university computer account names are easily stolen, and your name may be used to bamboozle others. Fortunately, many schools subscribe to electronic communications security services, such as Postini and Barracuda, that quarantine or remove most malware and spam. However, these services don't deal with spyware, which sends information about you back to the sender. Ask for both virus and spy protection for your computer at the office, and buy such protection for your home computer. They are wise investments. Most important, know about the problem and be careful.

169. DON'T GET ON TOO MANY E-MAIL LISTS. It is easy to join lots of e-mail lists that will bring you interesting news of your field from inside and outside academia. Like alcohol, e-mail lists should be used in moderation or not at all. Too many, and you waste your morning going through your e-mail rather than paying attention to teaching and research.

170. YOUR STUDENTS LOVE E-MAIL, TEXTING, AND TWITTER. It is a way for them to communicate with you directly whenever they feel the urge, day or night, rather than waiting for class or coming during office hours. They expect an instant response from you, whether it is midafternoon or three o'clock in the morning. Some expect you to act as if you were their slave. It is a bad student habit that can easily get out of hand.

Some faculty members we know tell their students they answer electronic communications only sporadically.

171. KEEP UP WITH COMPUTER DEVELOPMENTS. Wikis, blogs, instant voting and feedback, and course management software are four examples. Your students will often know about new computer tools before you or even your computer center people do, and they will expect you to know about them and use them.

- Wikis—The term *wiki* comes from Hawaiian and it means to do things quickly. A wiki is software that creates a public text forum that can be edited or added to by anyone with access to the Internet or to a school's local intranet. Wikis are extremely simple and easy to use by nontechnical people. For example, each student in a class can contribute material to a written discussion, submit homework, or receive information from the instructor or a teaching assistant. Using a wiki for homework discourages plagiarism among students because each student's work is seen by everyone else in the class.

- Wikipedia—Wikipedia (www.wikipedia.org) is a large wiki that contains an electronic encyclopedia, much larger than the *Encyclopedia Britannica*, freely available on the Internet. It is a marvelous place to obtain an introduction to almost any topic. Two caveats: (1) Because of its open authorship, Wikipedia can and does sometimes contain errors; and (2) your students may be tempted to plagiarize Wikipedia in their papers. It is wise to check Wikipedia to catch copying. (For more about Wikipedia, see Hint 98.)

- Blogs—The term *blog* comes from *Web log*. It refers to websites maintained by one or more individuals who create a diary with the most recent entry shown first rather than last and with the intent of being publicly available rather than private. Blogs are usually interactive so readers can make comments. Blogs can be on any subject, such as the material being covered in a class, politics, or simply personal records. You, as a faculty member, can maintain a blog for comment by your students and vice versa.

- Instant feedback and voting—Clickers, used in the classroom, are an example of instant feedback discussed in Hint 85.

- Course management software—Used by faculty and students, this software is designed to improve communication on what is required in a course and on its content. For a given course, students can find the syllabus, texts required and recommended, assignments, messages from faculty and other students, and chat rooms for studying jointly for exams. They also can be directed to material that expands on the course. Among many on the market, Blackboard and Moodle are perhaps the largest, most available management software packages used by colleges and universities. If you are moving to a new campus, find out which course management software is used there. It is prudent to obtain training on the software before you arrive, as you may be expected to start using it on the first day of class.

172. MEETINGS AND DIGITAL PUBLICATIONS. Become familiar with the digital aspects involved in proceedings' publishing and presentations at meetings. They're all done by e-mail. Even if you don't write for the electronic journals in your field, you will still use e-mail to

- submit your papers and revisions,
- receive review comments,
- receive letters of acceptance, and
- receive and send back proof copies.

You will find it easiest to set up separate folders for each paper. Also, use identification numbers or dates for each version you create so you can keep track of what is current and what is old.

173. INTERLIBRARY LOANS ARE QUICKER AND MORE EFFICIENT THAN THEY USED TO BE. For example, you can order reprints of journal articles delivered to your e-mail inbox. But you need to know the full reference to get what you want. We recommend *not* giving up going to the library to browse through the stacks; you will find articles and books there you didn't know existed. Note that many libraries are going digital. Theirs is a mailing list you want to be on.

174. USE DIGITAL COLLECTIONS IF THEY ARE AVAILABLE IN YOUR FIELD. Many professional organizations, particularly in the sciences, offer full paper access to all their publications, past and present, via the Internet. However, these collections may not be free and may not be available through your institution. Typically you must be a member of the professional organization and pay an annual fee. On the other hand, these collections are so vast and searchable that the fee is well worth it, whether you are primarily a researcher or a teacher.

175. TELECOMMUTING. Working away from the office was introduced about 40 years ago during the mainframe era in computing. It was a revolutionary concept.[2] In today's interconnected world, it is a reality. Students can contact you electronically, and you them, at any time (Hint 170), and you can collaborate with colleagues worldwide.

Particularly in your pre-tenure years, time is one of your most precious resources. Telecommuting from home lets you preserve your time. You must be on campus to meet your responsibilities for teaching, office hours, and committee meetings. You should also be in the office for some hours during the week to interact with colleagues. However, you can create blocks of telecommuting time to work off campus. As long as your telecommuting occurs at regular times, students will adjust to your schedule.

Be careful how you use your telecommuting time. Avoid Watson's syndrome (Hint 15) of procrastinating. If you have a family, be sure to set up a separate workspace for yourself and your computer where you are not disturbed. If you can't avoid interruptions at home, find quiet space elsewhere (e.g., the library).

176. YOUR WEBSITE. People who want to know about you and your work, including the 100 powerful people in your field (Hint 2), will first Google your name to find your website so they can learn about you. So will potential employers, peer reviewers of your grant proposals, and even reviewers of articles you submit (if they know or can deduce your name). Clearly, your Web presence should be outstanding.

Unless you have mastered website creation software, you should hire a specialist. It's worth the expense in the long term. In some schools, your department may cover this expense or support the development of a limited or skeletal Web presence for you and your work. In the latter case, develop an extensive personal website and link it to your institution's site.

You probably will need to buy a Web presence (domain name). Doing so is easy unless the domain name you prefer is already taken. Even so, you probably can register a similar name. If MarySmith .com is not available, try MaryBSmith.com or ProfMarySmith.com or DrMarySmith.com. Maintaining a domain name is quite inexpensive.

Your website should contain some or all of the following, along with a formal photograph:

- home page
- contact information
- a page about your teaching
- key publications
- current research projects
- a one-page professional biography (particularly useful for being introduced as a speaker)
- perhaps a more personal, informal narrative
- a list of your consulting clients if you consult
- a link to your full professional résumé

177. YOUR WEB VISIBILITY. Search engine specialists often refer to search engine optimization (SEO), a way to improve your website visibility in search engines. Let's say you are a specialist in health informatics who uses innovative technology to facilitate the effective use of medical information. If someone Googles *health informatics*, you want your work to pop up on the first page, preferably at or near the top. One strategy that can help you accomplish that goal is to start a blog about your work. The Google algorithm tracks how many times people visit a website. If you post items on your topical blog once or twice a week about, say, health informatics, and if you invite comments, you may develop followers. Each time one of them visits your site to read your latest missive, or to post a response, Google takes note. The visitor count is upped by 1. The more popular your website, the better a chance it has of appearing on the first page of Google search results.

178. THE PERSISTENCE OF LANGUAGE. Terms associated with digital media such as *slides* for PowerPoint and *turn the page* for e-books on Kindle and Nook are often vestigial remains from previous technologies. They are used with the current technology only because they provide a comfortable transition for adopters. The old terms remain in use because inventing and applying new names is a hassle. In academia, older faculty are more comfortable with the old terms. However, within seven years after introduction of a new use for an old term, freshmen no longer identify with the old meaning (Hint 94).

Institutional Citizen

As a member of the academic community, you are a citizen of the institution. You have obligations to the institution just as it has obligations to you.

179. GET TO KNOW THE DEVELOPMENT PEOPLE IN YOUR SCHOOL AND SUPPORT THEM.[3] At most institutions, members of the development department's administrative staff are charged with obtaining endowments and other gifts, maintaining relations with alumni, and so on. Skilled, interactive development officers can help in obtaining outside funding for you, for your department, and for students, all of which improves your quality of life. Be careful, however; development officers can be horribly inept. Their people are usually underpaid, and in this world you get what you pay for. Many are fund-raisers who know nothing about the academic enterprise or what you do. You will be educating them over and over. You may need to team up with colleagues to get people who are extremely ineffective replaced.

180. BE RESPONSIVE TO THE ALUMNI OFFICE just as you are to the development office. For many alumni, their college experience is the highlight of their lives, and the old school tie is one of the few things they can flaunt. They like to hear good things about their school because it makes their degree more valuable. If you are asked to write something for the alumni bulletin or give a speech, do it. Alumni can support their old department in a variety of ways. If they know you, they can support you from the outside at crunch time.

181. WHEN YOU DO SOMETHING NOTEWORTHY, LET YOUR SCHOOL'S PUBLIC RELATIONS DEPARTMENT KNOW, and ask that it be publicized. When you publish a book, win a prize, get elected to a professional society office, or do something in the community, get public relations into the act. It is one way for a lot of your colleagues across campus to find out what a wonderful person you are. (They may even remember it at promotion time!) It also provides you an opportunity to brag to your chairperson and the people in your department without being obnoxious about it.

182. COMMUNICATING YOUR FIELD TO THE PUBLIC. Those who can clearly communicate ideas from their discipline to the public hold an important place in our society. If you develop this skill, you can become a *public intellectual*. Some highly successful public intellectuals have included astronomer Carl Sagan of Cornell University, who had a television series; Daniel Patrick Moynihan of Harvard, who became a U.S. senator; and Stephen Jay Gould, also of Harvard, who was a widely published paleontologist and evolutionary biologist.

Listed by your school's PR department as an expert in your field, you can expect local (and sometimes national) media to ask for your comments. If you are good on TV, you will be asked about all kinds of topics, many beyond your expertise. Don't pontificate on subjects you know next to nothing about.

183. THE FACULTY SENATE IN MOST INSTITUTIONS PROVIDES A FORUM. Faculty are elected to the senate, usually by people in their department or their school. If elected, being a senator provides a way for you to communicate with the higher levels of administration on matters important to you and to your department. Senate election also increases your visibility. Be aware, however, that Faculty Senate work can eat up a large amount of your time. Our advice, therefore, is if you are asked to run, do so, providing you are tenured and your school's senate is not a collection of malcontents who are ignored by the administration.

184. SERVICE. The party line is that a junior professor seeking tenure should do well in research, teaching, and service. However, they are not equal in value. Service is the least important. One university president admonished new faculty members to earn an A in research, a B in teaching, and a D in service.

While "service" can include service to your community or city, and service to your discipline nationally, it usually involves serving on faculty committees. Do your share. Avoid being labeled a bad citizen, but do not extend yourself excessively.

Serving on some committees, such as the institutional review board (Hint 111) or a committee on which you are the technical expert, can be a time sump. In the case of the institutional review board, you have to read every research proposal, including student proposals, with a fine-tooth comb. If you know something about libraries, don't serve on the library committee. If you do, you will be assigned to the subgroup (or, worse, become the subgroup) to make recommendations or solve the mess in your area of expertise. You will lose valuable time with few visible results and even less personal gain for you. A good department chair or dean will protect you against such committee assignments until you have tenure. If you are uncertain about the time required for various committees, ask around.

Be sure to avoid service that not only takes time but also drags you into faculty politics. For example, don't get elected to the Faculty Executive Committee or the Faculty Senate until you are tenured.

Under no circumstances should you serve on a committee that is rewriting by-laws.

Department Chair

Department chairs will seem to be lofty people to you, having a job you think you should aspire to. It's not quite all wine and roses.

185. NEVER, EVER BECOME A DEPARTMENT CHAIR (EVEN AN ACTING DEPARTMENT CHAIR) UNLESS YOU'RE A TENURED FULL PROFESSOR. Yes, it will reduce your teaching load. Yes, it will give you visibility. Yes, you will be the first person contacted by an outside firm seeking a consultant. No, it will not confer power on you. The job carries with it some onerous burdens. First and foremost, most department chairs do less research and publish less while in that position than they would as a faculty member. Thus, you are producing less portable wealth per year (Hint 70), and you are reducing your chances for tenure or for promotion. The service you perform does not get you tenure. Don't feel flattered if the job is offered and you are pressured by the dean to accept it. What is really going on is that the dean has no other viable candidate who is willing to do it. If you must accept, realize you are in the same bargaining position as a new hire. The dean wants you badly. Use the opportunity to obtain something in return. If you are untenured, accept the job subject to the condition that you will be granted tenure in the next academic year; if you are an associate professor, insist on a promotion to full professor. Be clear beforehand that you will resign the chair's job if the agreement is broken, and if it is (as is often the case) follow through. As the advertisement says, deans operate on the principle of "Promise them anything, but give them . . ."

186. BE AWARE THAT THE POWERS OF A DEPARTMENT CHAIR ARE FEW. One of us wrote down the following seven absolute powers he had at a particular university:

- the right to attend meetings of the department chairs with the dean
- the right to chair meetings of the department
- the right to interview candidates for secretary
- the right (subject to a few side conditions) to select which classes he would teach and at which times
- the right to approve (or disapprove) student petitions
- the right to greet outside visitors to the department
- the right to resign as chair

187. THE ROLE CONFLICT IN THE JOB. You will spend a considerable amount of your time solving problems brought to you by your faculty colleagues. The faculty will want you to obtain goodies for them (space, computers, research money, reduced teaching loads, and on and on). On the other hand, the dean will want you to act as a first-line manager whose main role is to keep the bastards down so they cause no trouble.

The job is best characterized by these lines from Gilbert and Sullivan's *Gondoliers*:

> But the privilege and pleasure
> That we treasure beyond measure
> Is to run little errands for the Ministers of State!

188. LEADERSHIP. As a faculty member you will learn a lot about bad management by observing the various chairs, deans, and higher administrators. You will feel that any dolt could do better than they do, and you will often be right. At some point, however, management may become real for you if you are asked to become a department chair or an associate dean. Now you must provide leadership and avoid the traps your predecessors fell into. Management is a discipline that you can study and learn. Those people in the business school really do know something, and what they know is leadership. Like teaching, leadership is a learnable art.

189. DEALING WITH STUDENT PROBLEMS. If you do become department chair, know that most students who come into your office do so while in crisis. They are unhappy about a grade. They want to be exempted from a course or an examination. They need to explain they did not cheat even though their term paper was identical word for word to one submitted by another student the year before. You are the end of the line for them. You cannot throw them out. You need to listen and be firm but sympathetic at the same time. It takes a strong stomach and a feeling for people.

190. THE REDEEMING SOCIAL VALUES OF BEING CHAIR. Despite the foregoing caveats, being a department chair does have redeeming social values. If you have a vision of where you think the future of the department lies, you can use your moral suasion as chair to move people in the direction you believe is right. Notice we use the term *moral suasion*, not *power*. You need to develop a constituency for your ideas. In academia, Theory X management (I tell, you do) does not apply. Japanese Theory Z management (nothing happens until a consensus is reached) is the appropriate model.

191. DON'T STAY IN THE CHAIR POSITION TOO LONG. If you do, you become a victim of your past decisions. You become locked into doing what you did before, whether it is still the appropriate thing to do or not. Fortunately, unlike industry, you can keep pace if you step down and work for someone who previously worked for you. When you step down, don't second-guess your successors on every little point. They, like you before them, need all the help they can get.

Travel and Conferences

Although you can keep in contact with your field through reading books and journals, corresponding by e-mail, and hearing lecturers that come to your department, what you learn is limited. Dating back to the Royal Society of London in the 17th century, academics travel to conferences to expand their horizons by finding out and discussing what is new.

192. PROFESSIONAL TRAVEL. One of the least kept secrets of academia is that professors travel, subsidized by institutional and foundation funding, to interesting places and meet interesting people.[4]

Travel is a major fringe benefit. The amount of travel varies by field and by institution. In most fields, one or more major meetings a year take place at the national and regional levels. Despite financial stringencies, most institutions pay your way if you are on the program or involved in recruiting (usually restricted to senior faculty). Furthermore, each meeting is scheduled in a different location. Since it is easier to win approval for a short trip than it is for long trips, take the opportunity to attend nearby meetings whenever they occur.

For full-time graduate students, meetings are a little more difficult to attend because little funding is usually available and few graduate students are personally wealthy. Yes, students pay lower (usually much lower) registration fees, share rooms at a Days Inn or Motel Six, and for reasonable distances can carpool. Still, it is a financial stretch. If you're the best doctoral student close to a degree, you may be designated as your program's candidate for the doctoral consortium. You then must compete with candidates from other institutions for an available slot. If you win that lottery, you may get most or all of your expenses paid.

193. ATTEND CONFERENCES. Conferences in your professional specialty are held all the time. They become a significant part of your academic life that begins when you are a graduate student. Some are small, others huge. You should attend conferences whenever possible to gain the following advantages:

- You present your work to knowledgeable peers who provide valuable feedback.
- Like the players in an orchestra, you can tune your work. Is your work where the field is right now? Remember, journal articles report work that is more than a year old (Hint 234).

- You can hear and meet many of the 100 powerful people (Hint 2).
- You learn about new ideas, the hot new topics, and if you're astute, what is now passé. Like Sherlock Holmes in the *Hound of the Baskervilles*, you learn from what is not being barked at the meeting.
- You make new friends (the real kind, not the Facebook kind), and you can check out which colleges and universities are good places to work and which are not.
- You learn about the job market and who needs faculty, because schools recruit at larger conferences. If you are job hunting as an about-to-be PhD or looking for a better position, comparison shop just as recruiters comparison shop candidates.
- If there is a publisher's book fair, you find out about new books and texts.
- You learn about funding opportunities.

194. CHOOSING YOUR CONFERENCES. Choose conferences, particularly your first one, that relate closely to your dissertation, research, or teaching interests. Most fields use e-mail listservs to publicize meetings. You should get on their mailing lists.

At a national conference, the papers are more interesting but you may feel overwhelmed. Unless they are within driving distance, national conferences tend to be more expensive (travel, registration, hotel). Regional and graduate student conferences are lower cost and lower level in content but not as overwhelming.

195. ABSTRACTS HELP YOU GET ON CONFERENCE PROGRAMS. You apply to present at most conferences with an abstract, due well in advance. Prepare it carefully. If you're presenting work from your dissertation, edit the abstract so it applies to the conference theme. Create an abstract that grabs the program committee's interest.

Good abstracts are hard to write. Pay attention to them. Don't toss them off in an hour.

Be aware that meetings use up a chunk of your time. If your abstract is accepted, you will be asked to submit a paper, which again is due well before the conference. If the paper passes peer review and is accepted, you have a publication. Still you will need to proofread the paper, obtain funding to go, find people to cover your classes while you are away, spend as much as a day traveling in each direction, and spend additional days at the meeting. We won't even mention the hassles at airports.

196. YOUR CONFERENCE PRESENTATION. Rehearse your presentation, preferably in front of your friends and colleagues, before you leave for the conference. Most likely, your paper will be one of several in a session. You will be allocated 15 minutes, with perhaps 5 minutes for a senior person (called a *discussant*) to give you instant feedback.

Some conference presentations are superb. Learn from them. Others drone on and on and on. Your own performance will be judged by your audience. Stay within your time limit, and be at least as clear as when you teach a class.

If you are comfortable with PowerPoint (Hint 86), use it. Show only your main points on the slides.

Don't worry if one or two people walk out when you start your talk. When sessions are simultaneous, people sometimes switch to another paper they want to hear which is being presented at the same time as yours. However, if many people walk out while you talk, it's a bad sign.

197. PROTECT YOUR INTELLECTUAL CAPITAL WHILE TRAVELING. You can publish your research findings in a journal after you presented a paper on them at a conference. Be careful, however, not to present creative initial speculations and hypotheses you are not yet ready to publish. They can be stolen by unscrupulous members of your audience.

198. Drew's rule of conference redundancy. You can cite a previously published finding or one you presented at an earlier conference in a new and different context. But don't overdo it. Here is a good rule of thumb: If you found a correlation (a number between 0 and 1), multiply it by 10. That's how many years you can still discuss it.

For example, one of us discovered and reported in 1975 a correlation of 0.91 between (a) the prestige of graduate mathematics departments and (b) the rate at which their faculty published in the discipline's most highly cited journals. He was asked to discuss this finding at several conferences. He accepted the last such invitation in 1984.

Grievances

There comes a time in the life of students as well as faculty when they whine about the injustice of it all. As an academic you need to know about grievance procedures.

199. You may become involved in a student grievance at some point in your academic career. We are a litigious society, fueled in part by a supply of lawyers and in part by demand for equal treatment under the law. Fortunately, most universities and colleges have grievance procedures to handle disputes. We estimate that the chance of your being involved in a student grievance sometime during your academic career is 50%. Typically, these disputes are over grades, results of examinations, acts of cheating, and the like. Sometimes they are the result of delusions by students about their abilities. Other times they are the results of behavior on your part that a student perceives as insulting or demeaning.

200. SEXUAL HARASSMENT. The last decade saw the growth of sexual harassment as a basis for complaints. You may find yourself as the originator or the recipient of such a complaint. The source may be a student, a staff member, or another faculty member. Remember that harassment complaints can lead to litigation in court. Your institution may or may not be supportive. If it isn't, you can wind up spending large amounts on lawyers and court fees. The best strategy is preventive. Here are a few things you can do to protect yourself:

- Know and obey your institution's rules on harassment.
- Know what the procedures are for the offended party.
- Never meet with a student of either sex behind a closed door.[5]
- Never use language or examples that can be considered sexually offensive.

201. FACULTY RARELY VOLUNTEER TO SERVE ON THE GRIEVANCE COMMITTEE. It is not a pleasant duty. As a result, faculty are often appointed to this committee when they are not appropriate for other vacancies. Young faculty generally do not have the experience or skills of judges or dispute professionals. Like most judicial proceedings, the results involve a certain element of chance. Committees often fudge the outcome, particularly if the grievance is framed in a "she said, he said" form. Thus, even if you are completely in the right in a dispute, try to avoid using this committee. Furthermore, as a young faculty member, avoid serving on this committee if at all possible.

202. YOU MAY BECOME THE GRIEVANT AGAINST YOUR INSTITUTION. Disputes can arise over such issues as tenure; sabbatical entitlements; teaching loads; outrageous treatment by department chairs or deans; salaries; discrimination because of age, gender, or ethnicity; and more. The bad news is that many people will remember the incident negatively even when you win.

Dealing With Myths

When you talk with family, friends, and others who do not work in academia, don't be surprised to discover that they believe some of the standard myths about professors. The following hints deal with two of them.

203. MYTH 1: FACULTY ENJOY LOTS OF FREE TIME. "I envy all the free time you have. You mean you actually get paid for working 12 hours a week?" They may also tell you that old joke—*Question*: What does a professor say at the end of the work week? *Answer*: "Thank God it's Tuesday."

Actually, most professors work well over 40 hours per week, and that includes not only time spent on campus but also time working at home in the evenings and on weekends. If your department offers courses to students who are employed full-time, you will be on campus some nights until 9:00 or 10:00.

204. MYTH 2: FACULTY'S POLITICAL LEANINGS. "All professors are political leftists. Our universities are controlled by radicals and liberals."

Surveys show that the majority of professors are either conservative or middle of the road. You will discover that when it comes to changing their own behavior, your colleagues are unusually conservative and move very slowly. They follow Frank H. T. Rhodes's sardonic assertion "Never, under any circumstance, do something for the first time."[6]

Notes

1. In some places, computing is outsourced. However, it requires lots of local staff to actually run the computer center.

2. See J. Nilles, F. Carlson, P. Gray, and G. Hanneman, *Telecommunications-Transportation Tradeoffs: Options For Tomorrow* (New York: John Wiley & Sons, 1976).

3. *Development* is an old-fashioned term. Many of the larger schools use the more fashionable word *advancement*. Ironically, most advancement campaigns begin with a retreat for faculty.

4. However, if you are traveling abroad, many institutions will only pay for you to travel to the farthest U.S. point.

5. Some of our colleagues believe this advice is too stringent. They argue that when a student requests privacy, it calls for a closed door. We disagree. Privacy can be achieved as easily by walking with the student to a quiet food area or other public space.

6. Rhodes is president emeritus of Cornell University. He made this statement at the 1997 opening of the Keck Graduate Institute. He referred to it as the "cardinal law of academic governance."

11

DIVERSITY

HINT 205: THE CONTINUING GOAL. Although you may hear that universities are leaning over backward to hire women and minorities, such cases are exceptions and are rare.

THE PERVASIVENESS OF DIVERSITY in the general population in the United States does not yet apply to the American professoriate. This statement is not surprising, given that most of the faculty currently serving in academia were hired at a time in the previous century when diversity was only talked about but was not practiced. Diversity, in our view, reflects the presence of women and men; people whose ethnic roots may be from Europe, Africa, Asia, and the Western Hemisphere; disabled people; and more. To simplify our discussion, we concentrate on women and people of color. However, our points are applicable to all groups.[1]

All the hints in this chapter apply to new faculty members but perhaps more so to women faculty and faculty of color. Whereas portions of this book take a lighthearted view of many aspects of academe, in this chapter we are deadly serious. To us, the authors, diversity is an important goal and one that is still far from being realized. We quote research results and we try to dispel some of the myths that surround the subject.

The reality of the situation is evident in the following quotation:

> The search and hiring process continues largely unchanged. The lack of diversity on search committees continues to limit the potential for introducing new perspectives to the process of evaluation.
>
> The climate for faculty of color in institutions remains uncomfortable and difficult, regardless of the circumstances under which the individual was hired.[2]

To learn more about the state of diversity, read the growing literature by women, minority, and disabled scholars about the academic world. For example, Gail Thompson and Angela Louque combined statistical analysis of survey data from a sample of African American faculty members with interview data.[3] The picture they paint is not always pretty. When asked about the most difficult aspects of life in the academy, survey respondents cited the low number of faculty of color and the racial climate. Like other faculty members, they also mentioned issues we address in these hints: time for research, time management, time for course preparation, and the teaching load. For additional sources, see the endnotes following this chapter.

205. THE CONTINUING GOAL. Although you may hear universities are leaning over backward to hire women and minorities, such cases are exceptions and are rare. Based on a review of the data we were able to find and on the experiences of junior professors we know, these claims are not supported.

In response to increasing concern over the lack of diversity in universities, some improvement has occurred, but it has been at the margins. For example, between 1993 and 2003, the percentage of underrepresented minority faculty "grew from 6.8% to 7.2% within the University of California system" and grew roughly from 6% to 8% nationally at four-year institutions.[4] Do not expect that a 0.4% increase (if you seek employment in the University of California system) or even 2% represents a sea change in the college or university culture. The University of California employed 8,200 tenure-track faculty in 2005.[5] So we are talking about a net increase on the order of 30 to 40 positions for the University of California system over a 10-year period. For four-year colleges, the full-time instructional faculty was 626,000 in 1993.[6] A 2% change would indicate about 13,000 positions. Although this number is nontrivial, it translates on average to a total of 10 to 15 positions over 10 years at an institution.

206. VARIATIONS AMONG INSTITUTIONS. What should you do if you fall into the underrepresented minority category? Diversity varies greatly among institutions. When considering an offer, and even when making an application, try to find out whether the institution you are considering as your future intellectual home shows a genuine openness and commitment to supporting and mentoring all junior faculty, including women and people of color. A massive study of attempts by universities to diversify their faculty concluded, "Campuses with greatest gains had explicitly connected their efforts to their educational mission and had implemented multiple strategies to improve the recruitment and selection process with regard to [underrepresented minority] candidates."[7]

207. ASSESSING COLLEAGUES AND DEANS. When looking for your first job or changing jobs, try to assess how open and supportive an institution is to diversity issues, and assess to the best of your ability your future department colleagues and your future dean. As we said in Hint 145, don't assume you can outwait a bad dean.

Given a Hobson's choice, it is better to take a position at the institution of your second choice if it has a supportive culture (even if its academic reputation is slightly lower) than at your top choice if you conclude you will encounter sexism or racism.

208. INDICATORS OF TRUE DIVERSE HIRING. An analysis of roughly 700 faculty searches concluded that underrepresented minority faculty are more likely to be hired at predominantly white institutions when the job description "explicitly engages diversity, . . . an institutional 'special hire' strategy is used," or when an "ethnically diverse search committee" is referred to.[8] This research provides clues to help you sort through job possibilities. Check if the advertisement for the position stresses diversity, and look at the ethnic makeup of the search committee.

209. THE CLIMATE FOR WOMEN IN ACADEMIA has improved more than the climate for people of color, but we still are a long way from full equity. Women still encounter extra obstacles and chillier climates at each step up the academic ladder. Yes, women are now presidents of Ivy League schools. Yes, women dominate the numbers in some fields. However, the firestorm in 2005 over remarks by the former president of Harvard University, Lawrence Summers, about the possible genetic inferiority of women for work in the sciences and engineering highlighted how far we still have to go in academia.

On some campuses women belong to formal support groups. For example, on one campus a Female Faculty Forum was created as a reaction to perceived unresponsiveness from the administration. The female faculty meet once a month to discuss policy issues and politics at the university, to share concerns, and to support one another.

210. DISABILITIES. Diversity includes disability. We hope your university facilitates access for disabled students and professors, including, for example, ramps for wheelchairs and websites accessible to the visually impaired.[9] Some types of disabilities require accommodation from you. For example, give more time on examinations to students with dyslexia or other learning disabilities. Accommodation is not only good policy, it is the law (Americans With Disabilities Act of 1990).

If you are disabled, carefully study how a prospective employer addresses your disabilities. Some institutions are more welcoming than others.

211. WORKLOAD FOR UNDERREPRESENTED FACULTY. If you are a member of an underrepresented group, you may find you are the only member of this group (or one of two people) in your department, school, or university. For example, you may be the only African American or the only Latino/Latina in the psychology department, or the only woman in engineering or the only man in a nursing program.

Be prepared for extra work. Many African American or Latino/Latina students probably will seek you out as a teacher and mentor. You will be asked to join many faculty committees.

Ultimately, your comfort level, feeling of community, and productivity will be strongly affected by whether your department or institution truly values and respects diversity.

Notes

1. Our definition of *diversity* applies to faculty, students, curriculum, and research topics. In this chapter, we concentrate on faculty, particularly newly hired faculty. Also, in this chapter we consider underrepresentation in predominantly white, coeducational institutions. While an important part of academia, institutions such as historically black colleges and universities (e.g., Howard) and historically women's colleges (e.g., Scripps) are not explicitly discussed here.

2. From D. G. Smith, L. E. Wolf, B. Busenberg, and associates, *Achieving Faculty Diversity: Debunking the Myths. A Research Report of a National Study* (Washington, DC: Association of American Colleges and Universities, 1996).

3. G. Thompson and A. Louque, *Exposing the "Culture of Arrogance" in the Academy: A Blueprint for Increasing Black Faculty Satisfaction in Higher Education* (Sterling, VA: Stylus, 2005).

4. J. F. Moreno, D. G. Smith, A. R. Clayton-Pedersen, S. Parker, and D. H. Teraguchi, *The Revolving Door for Underrepresented Minority Faculty in Higher Education: An Analysis from the Campus Diversity Initiative* (San Francisco, CA: James Irvine Foundation, 2006), 2.

5. M. A. Mason, A. Stacy, M. Goulden, C. Hoffman, and K. Frasch, *University of California Family Friendly Edge: An Initiative for Tenure Track Faculty at the University of California*, (2005), http://ucfamilyedge.berkeley.edu/ucfamilyedge.pdf.

6. *Digest of Educational Statistics* (Washington, DC: Institute of Educational Sciences, U.S. Department of Education, 2004).

7. Moreno et al., *The Revolving Door*, pp. 7–8.

8. D. G. Smith, C. S. V. Turner, N. Osei-Kofi, S. Richards, "Interrupting the Usual: Successful Strategies for Diversifying the Faculty," *Journal of Higher Education* 75, no. 2 (2004).

9. W. Smith, "Assessing the Minimal Conformance with Web Accessibility and Technical Recommendations for Universities and Colleges in California" (unpublished dissertation, Claremont Graduate University, March 2008).

12

ON WRITING

HINT 212: LEARN HOW TO WRITE CLEARLY.

TEACHING, RESEARCH, AND WRITING are the three activities academics engage in most. Writing manuscripts—research papers, books, or class notes—requires specialized skills. Here are some thoughts about writing. Publishing what you write is discussed in Chapter 13.

212. LEARN HOW TO WRITE CLEARLY. Some graduate programs do their best to stamp out this skill, persuading doctoral candidates that a ten-syllable word is better than a two-syllable word. Reviewers are more likely to persevere to the end of your journal submission or your grant proposal if they can easily follow what you say. They are also more likely to give you a favorable review. If all else fails, use the style of these hints and the writing tips in Appendix D.

213. LEARN THE FINE POINTS OF ENGLISH. With multiple degrees in hand, you are assumed to be an educated person. Writing and speaking mistakes turn off your students, reviewers, and editors of journals.

If you need help, buy *Pocket Fowler's Modern English Usage* and William Strunk Jr. and E. B. White's *The Elements of Style*.[1] Read them. When in doubt, consult them. Remember, a well-written paper is more likely to be accepted than a poorly written one.

For example, you should

- know the difference between *assure*, *ensure*, and *insure*, and between *affect* and *effect*; and
- recognize that *criteria* is plural and *criterion* is singular.

To help you with your writing, Appendix D presents a series of simple hints to make your prose sparkle. Absorb them now. Go back to them when you finish a draft for submittal, and apply the principles as you edit the manuscript.

214. Be sure to spell-check, grammar-check, and fact-check your work. Your degrees certify you as a literate, educated person. Grammatical or spelling errors in a résumé or in an article submitted for publication turn off reviewers who are making judgments about you. For example, in a résumé sent to one of us as an outside reviewer for tenure, we found the following: "My research activities has centered on . . ." and a reference to the journal *Group Decision and Negotiation* wound up as *Group Decision & Negation*.

215. Editing your own material. As you write your dissertation or paper it is natural to make changes and major revisions. You are, in effect, editing your own material. That's good and bad. It is good because you add intellectual capital, you clarify, and you consider the knowledge (or lack thereof) of your readers. It is bad if, like most of us, you become infatuated with the sound of your own words. It is difficult, if not impossible, to change language or ideas you labored over long and hard.

Just like job application letters, have at least one person (preferably more) read what you wrote and suggest improvements. If a word, a paragraph, or a section is unclear to any of them, then it is likely to be unclear to others. It's better to receive critiques and suggested improvements from your peers than from referees or decision makers.

216. Limits on self-plagiarism. Although plagiarism is a no-no (Hint 114), under some circumstances you can appropriately integrate the published text of one of your old findings in a new publication if it is relevant. But do not base very much of the new manuscript on text you published previously unless it is relevant.

217. CITATIONS. When you write a paper, you cite other researchers who preceded you. Once your paper is published, other scholars will cite you. Forty years ago, the Institute for Scientific Information developed software to count how many times an article was cited. Today that technology is incorporated in Google Scholar.

Your article citation counts are an important part of your academic record. You are more likely to be cited if you publish in a leading journal (Hint 127). Because the software can filter out self-citations, you can't boost your numbers simply by repeatedly citing yourself.

We knew a distinguished scholar who applied a new analytical technique but made a mistake. After that, other researchers cited him, warning, "Be sure not to do what Jones (not his real name) did." Jones, however, wound up with an impressively high citation score.

If you write the first paper that has been written in an area (Hint 224), you might reach the enviable position where others believe that citing your article is almost mandatory.

218. DEVELOP A POOL OF RESEARCH REFERENCES STORED IN YOUR COMPUTER.[2] Creating this pool is one of the most useful things you can do. You will use the same references over and over as you do research, as you write papers, and as you teach. You will add to this list as you read new articles and books in the literature. We personally recommend the software package EndNote, although other similar kinds of software are on the market.[3] Software for references contains three useful features:

- It provides a standard form for entering references so you remember to include all the necessary data. Separate forms are provided for each type of reference (e.g., books, articles, newspapers, Internet URLs).

- It automatically converts the format to the reference style of a particular journal. Lots of different styles are available. Since you may be sending an article to several journals sequentially before it is accepted (see Hint 4), this automated feature saves you hours of drudge work in converting reference formats.
- It provides space for including abstracts and notes so you can record what the reference was about for future retrieval.

219. REUSE THE LITERATURE SEARCH FROM YOUR DISSERTATION. If you conducted a thorough literature search for your dissertation, you will never need to do one again if you write in the same area. If you write in an adjacent field or on an adjacent topic or want to include the latest reference, your cycle time for the literature search is much, much shorter. Remember too that your students or graduate assistants will perform some of the slogging necessary for a literature search.

220. DEADLINES ARE FRIENDS, NOT ENEMIES. Many graduate students and professors hate deadlines even though they pervade academic life. If your dissertation isn't completed and approved by a specific date, you do not march at graduation. Requests for proposals require submission by a date certain. Book publishers' contracts and professional meetings set deadlines for submitting a polished draft. Grades are due shortly after the end of the semester or trimester. The list goes on.

The truth is that deadlines are friends, not enemies. They force you to finish and free your mind to move on to the next task. We know academics who lament that were it not for a deadline, their article or proposal would be much, much better. We doubt that. We estimate that three additional months spent on an article or proposal improves a manuscript by, at most, 15%. It's better to complete an excellent paper than to never finish the perfect paper.

Notes

1. R. Allen, ed., *Pocket Fowler's Modern English Usage* (New York: Oxford University Press, 2006); W. Strunk Jr. and E. B. White, *The Elements of Style,* 4th ed. (New York: Longman, 1999).

2. Be sure to keep a separate copy of this list in a removable drive or in printed form. Computer storage has been known to crash occasionally.

3. For more information on EndNote, go to http://www.endnote.com.

13

ON PUBLISHING

HINT 229: PUBLISH "EARLY AND OFTEN."

A T SEVERAL POINTS along the way to this chapter, we stressed the need for you to publish if you are going to survive in a research-oriented institution. In this section (and in the subsections on journals and on book publishers), we present what you need to know about the publication process. Also, go back to Hint 4 (Drew's law), which tells you every good paper can find a home.

221. SUBMIT YOUR PAPERS TO THE BEST JOURNALS IN THE FIELD. (There is an exception: don't send stinkers to these journals. They will remember and will even automatically reject your subsequent good work.) If a paper is rejected, work your way down the list. Many articles rejected by a poor journal were later accepted by a leading journal, so you might as well start with the best. It is easier to follow this rule if you are thick-skinned.

Two additional factors should affect where you place a journal on your go-to list: (a) the percentage of submitted papers the journal accepts and (b) the length of time it takes the journal to review a submission. Not all journals make this information public.

222. WRITE MOST OF YOUR PAPERS FOR REFEREED JOURNALS. Papers presented at meetings get you funds to be a world traveler. However, even if refereed, conference papers don't really count for tenure, promotion, or salary raises.

223. AVOID WRITING INTRODUCTORY TEXTBOOKS if you are not tenured. You can make a lot of money (Hint 273), although many of these books wind up taking so much time you would be financially better off if you had worked for minimum wage at McDonald's. Most tenure committees think of them as moonlighting, not scholarly productivity.

Your colleagues will assume you write text for the money (called "dirty money" by some), which allows you to live in a better house and wear better clothes than they do. This attitude is particularly evident in those who took a vow of poverty (implicitly) when they joined academe. If you're a senior professor whose book sells, you will be praised for enhancing the department's reputation as well as your own (Hint 3). However, the jealousy will still be there.

224. RECOGNIZE THE DIFFERENCE BETWEEN WRITING THE FIRST PAPER ON A SUBJECT AND WRITING THE NTH ONE. Writing the first paper requires a special knack for originality, which few people have. A first paper usually is not very deep, but it creates enough of an impact that others will follow your lead and write deeper scholarly works. The advantage of the first paper is that it is always referenced, giving you a long list of citations. If you are fortunate enough to have the knack, you will need to market your output carefully. Journals (and reviewers) look for the tried and true. Journals, after all, publish almost exclusively on subjects they published previously. Members of tenure and promotion committees will read your paper and say it is trivial because they also read the more careful articles others wrote later based on your idea. It has been our observation that people who write first papers possess a different set of skills from those who write the nth ones, and should leave the writing of the nth papers to someone else.

225. WRITING THE NTH PAPER MEANS that $n - 1$ papers on the subject were written before yours. Although you need not cite all of them, you should cite enough of them so authors of previous papers will be selected as reviewers. (One of the secrets of the journal editor business is that editors find reviewers by looking in the reference lists for names of people they know.) You may, however, be unfortunate enough that someone you did not cite is selected to review your article. If so, the reviewer will probably comment that you failed to include the citation, which, of course, is a dead giveaway of the reviewer's name.[1]

226. WHEN WRITING THE *N*TH PAPER, MAKE YOUR CONTRIBUTION TO THE ISSUE CLEAR. Whether your contribution is a carefully conducted experiment or an elaboration of the theory or a synthesis and interpretation of previous work, be explicit in saying it. Reviewers need to be convinced the manuscript contains something new that merits publishing.

227. REVISE PAPERS QUICKLY. As an author, you don't help the publication process if you take a long time between receiving reviews and submitting the revised manuscript.

228. TURN YOUR REVIEWS OF OTHER PEOPLE'S PAPERS AROUND QUICKLY. Reviewing is both a scarce resource and important work. You want your work reviewed quickly, and you should show the same courtesy to others. Don't be too busy to review. Complete your review quickly.

229. PUBLISH "EARLY AND OFTEN," AS THEY SAY IN CHICAGO POLITICS. N matters, even though $N + 2$ is required for tenure (see Hint 1). If possible, begin writing for publication while you are still in graduate school. Data shows that people who publish while still in graduate school usually continue to publish at a faster rate after they graduate than those who didn't publish while still a student. Furthermore, published papers and monographs help you get your first job.

230. YOUR DISSERTATION IS A PUBLISHING ASSET. You should receive a return on your investment for the time and money spent in creating this asset. In the humanities, it should lead to at least one book or monograph. In the social sciences and the sciences, at least two papers should result. We recommend that, as a rule of thumb, one of these papers should be single-author, the other joint with your major adviser. Your major adviser put intellectual capital into the dissertation just as you did, and the joint publication is one way you can repay the adviser for the hours spent poring over your work and helping you over the tough intellectual hurdles. You should agree on this arrangement with your adviser before starting on your dissertation. Avoid advisers who insist on joint authorship with you on all papers that result from your dissertation. They are exploiting you.

231. THE LITERATURE SEARCH YOU PERFORMED FOR YOUR DISSERTATION IS A TREASURE TROVE of information. It should be the foundation of a survey article on the field. And the world desperately needs more survey articles. Unfortunately, although only a few journals (e.g., *Computer Surveys*) accept such articles, you receive little credit for them in tenure and promotion reviews. You will be rewarded more for adding one little new data point to the literature than for a brilliant synthesis of that literature (unless your name is Arnold J. Toynbee). You can, however, transform a literature review into a meta-analysis, which is a systematic, statistical aggregation of previously published research findings. Such a paper carries more cachet with tenure committees, and the statistics are not difficult to compute.

232. INCLUDE SINGLE-AUTHOR PAPERS IN YOUR PORTFOLIO. Review committees wonder about people who always publish with someone else. Did they do the work or did they ride the coauthor's coattails?

Were they the first author? If you must coauthor, pick people whose names follow yours alphabetically and then suggest that your name really belongs first. (Choosing the order by flipping a coin, as was done for this book, is not recommended.) If you are unfortunate enough to be named Zyzygy, go to court and get it changed.

233. COAUTHORING A PAPER WITH A SUPERSTAR increases your visibility and associates you with his or her reputation. However, be careful which papers you coauthor. If the idea is yours, the superstar will likely get most of the credit.

234. BE AWARE OF THE DELAYS IN PUBLISHING. You face long, long delays. In this hint we estimate the delays in journal publication. For books, the total time is usually much longer. Let's assume you've written your first article and printed out a copy that is ready to send off to the top journal in the field. If you expect that this brilliant piece will appear in the next issue or, at the latest, the one after that, we have a bridge to sell you in Brooklyn. Let's assume your paper is so good it is accepted without a request for even minor revisions. Even in this unusual case, the pace of publication is extremely slow. To help you understand the time delays, we've created Tables 13.1, 13.2, and 13.3 that show the work flows. (If there was ever a process that needs reengineering, it is this one!) Note that Table 13.1 shows your paper has not yet been sent to a reviewer, and a month or more has passed.

If you add up the time periods for Steps 1 through 7 in Tables 13.1 and 13.2, the typical time it takes to get a decision is nearly six months. We are very generous in this best-case assessment; in real life, longer periods are not at all unusual.

At this point you can claim publication if the paper is accepted. If revision is required, you need to add the time you take to revise, the time the reviewers spend agreeing that the revisions meet their

TABLE 13.1
Work Flow in Periodicals Publishing

Step	By	Time Required
1. Produce copy of the article, prepare cover letter, e-mail	You and your department staff	1 week
2. Acknowledge receipt (publishers get a lot of submissions)	Editor's office	1 week
3. Decide who is to review	Editor	1 week to 4 weeks*
4. Article sent to two reviewers	Editor's staff	1 week

*Some editors work in batch mode. They let articles pile up for a while and then work on a group of them over a convenient weekend when it is raining or snowing outside.

standards, and exactly the same delays in mailing and writing e-mails as for the original draft. We leave it, as the mathematicians say, as "an exercise for the reader" to compute the delay if one, two, or three revisions are required.

But you're not the proud possessor of your name in print yet. There are a few more steps involved, as we show in Table 13.3.

Many of the numbers in the printing process are quite broad. For example, if a journal is published quarterly, an extra three months' delay may come just from your being the $N + 1$st article for an issue of N articles.

235. REWARDS FOR ACADEMIC PUBLISHING. The old saw "Virtue is its own reward" applies to most academic publications. There are exceptions. For a scholarly monograph in the humanities or the social sciences, you will receive a small royalty. Journals invariably

TABLE 13.2
Time to Decision

Step	By	Time Required
5. Review time	Reviewers	4 months
Most reviewers are senior people who are asked to review a lot of manuscripts. One colleague of ours totaled up the number he reviewed in a particular year and found it was 73. A good reviewer turns a submission around in weeks; a poor reviewer can take months. We won't even talk about the lowlifes who take a year. We estimate the median time to be three months.	Note that it is equally likely that a reviewer will take more or less time than the median. Remember that the time required for the review process is determined by the *slowest* reviewer.	The probability that both reviewers take less than the median time is 0.25; thus the review time for your manuscript will probably be longer than the median.
6. E-mail to editor	Reviewers	1 week
7. Accept/reject decision and e-mail to author on decision	Editor	1 week

do not pay. Your annual review to determine whether you should receive a raise, however, tends to reward you for publishing, particularly in highly reputed journals. Of course, if you work abroad in a school such as one we know about in South Korea, you may be awarded a bonus every time you publish, with the size of the bonus depending on the prestige of the journal.

Journals

You rely on journals as outlets for your work. Your relationship with a journal can also include your becoming an editor or a reviewer.

TABLE 13.3
Production Time for Accepted Journal Manuscripts

Step	By	Time Required
1. Manuscript is put in the queue for publication.	Editor	None
2. Depending on the backlog, the manuscript is sent to the compositor.	Editor	1 month
3. Manuscript is typeset.	Printer	2–4 weeks
4. Manuscript (now called "the *galley*") is sent back to you for final proof.	Printer, editor	1 week
5. The galley is proofread and mailed back to editor.	You	1–2 weeks
6. If submitted to a journal, manuscript is assigned to an issue.	Editor	No time
7. Manuscript is printed and the issue is bound.	Printer	1 month to 2 years depending on backlog
8. Issue is mailed out. You receive an author's .pdf copy of your article.*	Printer, editor	2–4 weeks

*Authors used to receive a copy of the complete journal issue or a printed copy even if they did not order reprints. Most publishers today merely send a .pdf copy of the printed version via e-mail.

236. Don't become an editor too early. That is, don't accept the impressive title *editor in chief* or *department editor* of any publication early in your career. Journal editing takes time. Don't get involved at the editorial level until your career is well launched. At all costs, avoid editing struggling newsletters, special-interest publications, and the like.

237. Do serve as a reviewer for journals, particularly top journals. Treat this job seriously. You will see much junk being submitted and appreciate why some journals reject 80% or more of their submissions. You will develop a sense of what is good and what is not. You will correspond with some powerful people (Hint 2). When you do get a good paper to review, you will receive much earlier knowledge of an important new development; the information you gain is worth more than the time you take to review it.

Book Publishers

Although the Internet and multimedia are here, the foreseeable future will still include textbooks and monographs. Book publishers are like honeybees. They bring the intellectual pollen you need for your classes. Publishers are outlets for your books (but see Hint 223 about the trade-off in writing textbooks).

238. Pay attention to the book publishers' representatives who come to your office. They are a valuable source of information. These reps have two missions: to flog the books their company issues and to send intelligence back to the home office. They will be pleased to send you complimentary copies of the latest mass market elementary textbooks in your field. If your field is French, you can obtain many shelves of freshman- and sophomore-level French books. You can also obtain copies of books directly linked to specific courses you teach. It is a little more difficult (but not impossible) to obtain complimentary copies of books in your research area. There's always the chance that you will adopt one of these for a course. Don't, however, simply look at the reps as a source of freebies. Use them to find out what is going on in the book market. Sound them out on whether their company is interested in a book manuscript you have under way. Their response will usually be positive. Ignore that. Just make sure they get the word about your forthcoming manuscript back to the editors at the publisher's headquarters.

239. SELECTING A PUBLISHER INVOLVES TRADE-OFFS. With a large publisher that issues many books in your field in a year, you gain the advantage of mass marketing and advertising. Large publishers employ reps who visit campuses. However, these reps are given many books to push, and their commissions depend on the number of books sold. As a result, they concentrate on freshman and sophomore texts for required courses. Furthermore, since they receive the same commission no matter which book they sell, they have little incentive to sell a particular book. Thus, you run the risk that the promotion of your book will be lost among the many others with similar titles being offered by that publisher. Small and specialty commercial publishers and university presses give you much more individual attention. You can judge whether they are a good fit for your book by looking at their publications list on their websites, the mailings you receive from them, the advertisements in your professional journals, and the experience and recommendations of your peers. If a publisher looks reasonable based on these probes, go to your school's library and look at its books. Before signing a contract, make sure your publisher will have your manuscript peer reviewed, and that the publisher you chose counts with your field's tenure committee. Under *no* circumstances publish with a vanity press, that is, a company that charges you for publishing your book.

240. GET TO KNOW THE MAJOR EDITORS of the book publishers in your field. The best place to meet them is at the book exhibits at your annual professional conferences. You will find that some of them know absolutely nothing about your field, not to mention your subject. Avoid working with such editors; they will treat your work as a commodity, like pork bellies.

Note

1. Some argue you should cite everyone who ever wrote on the subject. This approach is not desirable and often not feasible. If the subject is well published, you can never be certain you found every (obscure) reference, and your list of references would be extremely long—and too long a list may be held against you. It's better to take your chances on finding the relevant references and citing those.

14

PERSONAL
CONSIDERATIONS

HINT 246: LEARN TIME MANAGEMENT.

THE HINTS IN THIS CHAPTER refer to your actions as an individual.

241. LEARN NEW THINGS OVER TIME. Universities are notorious for not spending money on faculty development. Administrators assume that because you earned a PhD you learned all you will ever need to know. They are not consumers of their own educational product. Actually, you know the most about your field the week you take the prelims for the PhD (Hint 252). Thereafter, you tend to specialize and learn more and more about the narrower and narrower subfield you work in. But it is unfortunately true that fields change over time. Some subspecialties are mined out, and new results become ever more difficult to obtain. Other subspecialties make rapid strides that require you to learn new methodologies and become aware of a flood of literature. Some new technologies, such as computer-based retrieval, come along and change the research skills you need. If something new is important to your research, try to get your department to spring for some education. It may be a short course offered by the leading expert in the field or a tutorial offered at a professional meeting. If the time needed is sufficiently long, arrange your next sabbatical at one of the centers where the new knowledge is being developed.

242. SEQUENTIAL CAREERS. As a graduate student you may aspire to be the best professor of French or biology or sociology ever known. The reality, however, is that your interests and your circumstances will likely change. New topics arise, subfields stagnate or disappear, colleagues ask you to collaborate and cooperate, doctoral students ask you to serve on their committee on a topic, you start teaching a new course, or you take your sabbatical in a new environment.

In talking with your professors while you are a graduate student and later with your colleagues you will find that some well-respected individuals reached their current position serendipitously. For example, one of the authors of this book was a lead programmer at a famous university, a senior analyst for a Washington think tank, a statistician, a professor in the social sciences, and for a number of years, a dean. The other worked as a scientific editor, a large-scale systems researcher, department chair, and wrote first papers in three different fields. Each career change involved its own logic. For both of us, what we learned previously proved to be a foundation for the stages that followed.

Bottom line: Don't be afraid to tackle new directions. You can change what you do.

243. BEING AN EXPERT WITNESS. One day the phone will ring and you will be asked by a lawyer to be an expert witness. The attorney will tell you that all you need to do is help prepare the technical material in your specialty (which is fun) and to appear in court to swear to your findings. An ethical attorney will offer you a fixed fee or a fixed rate rather than ask you to bet on the contingency that your side will win. It looks like easy money, but it isn't really that simple. The legal culture is different from your field's culture. You will need to bridge the two-culture gap; lawyers won't and can't. You will have to teach the attorneys about your field. If you are a scientist, you will blanch at the low level of proof offered in court cases, and you will be appalled at the level of statistics being cited. When you do get to court, you will find you spend much of your time waiting around. Waiting is not bad; you are getting paid a premium for every hour spent in court. When it does come time to take the stand, your side's lawyer will lead you through a carefully rehearsed set of questions. Then the fun begins. The other side's lawyer will cross-examine you. The operative word is *cross*. That lawyer will try to find inconsistencies in what you said. The opposing side will try to twist your words to be favorable to its client. The other attorney will try to impugn your expertise, your honesty, your veracity. You can come out with a very jaundiced view of jurisprudence. The whole process will eat up a large chunk of your time, and if you are an untenured professor, remember that the income, like the summer teaching option (Hint 264) carries with it a big opportunity cost—the time lost working on your research. The work for a court case is almost never the basis of something publishable. Tenure committees view being an expert witness as a public service or consulting income, not professional work no matter how complex the case. If you do become a regularly employed expert witness, your initial choice of sides can quickly become permanent. If you are hired, say, by a plaintiff seeking psychic pain and suffering awards in an auto accident case one day, you will not credibly be able to represent an insurance company defendant the next.

You should conduct your analyses with integrity and report your findings with candor. However, this ethical approach may cost you some expert witness income. If the attorney doesn't like your findings from your background work, he or she won't ask you to testify in court and may not hire you for the next case.

244. WHISTLE-BLOWING. Every so often you will observe a situation in your department or your institution that you believe is not right. The situation might involve overpromising or underperforming by an administrator, or downright dishonesty (e.g., changing a grade you gave or taking bribes). A natural response is to become a whistle-blower. It is a response we respect and is in keeping with academic freedom.

Be aware, however, that whistle-blowing involves considerable risk. Yes, there is satisfaction in speaking up in a meeting or writing a letter to the local newspaper exposing the unethical deed. But the people involved will try to squelch you or retaliate if they can. They can remember at tenure time. They can try to have you fired. They can try to ruin your reputation. None of these outcomes is desirable. If the infraction is minor, we recommend you note it in your head for future reference. If it is major, start talking with people you absolutely trust. Build a coalition rather than being out front on your own.

245. DON'T BE A PENNY-ANTE THIEF. It may be awfully tempting to put personal correspondence in official envelopes, to use department secretaries to type your private letters, or to make personal long-distance calls. Don't do it. And don't use department funds to buy software or journal subscriptions to support your consulting practice. To paraphrase Abe Lincoln, you can get away with some of it all the time, and you can get away with all of it some of the time, but you can't get away with all of it all of the time. Don't develop a reputation of being someone who only takes not gives, of not having ethical respect for your colleagues or your institution.

246. LEARN TIME MANAGEMENT. First, finish reading this book. Then determine your work priorities and try as best you can to match your time commitments to those priorities.

The model of an academic having large blocks of time at work to think deeply about a problem is not real and may never have been. Your time on campus is fragmented. You get interrupted for teaching, office hours, supervising dissertations, phone calls, keeping up with e-mail, research, writing, publishing, and more. All of these activities are important or mandatory. You barely have time to be collegial (Hint 151).

If you become overloaded, use time management tools. The simplest is the calendar that comes with e-mail software. Keep a record not only of your appointments and your teaching commitments but also your interruptions. Analysis will show when you can combine repetitive interruptions and when you can undertake reading, research, and professional activities.

Learn to say *no*! One of our colleagues, who published well over 30 books in his career, said, "If you write only a page a day, that's a book a year." For more, read Alan Lakein's marvelous, short guide to time management.[1]

247. THE MEANING OF YOUR WORK WILL CHANGE OVER TIME. Whether you pursue multiple careers (Hint 242) or stay in one subject area at one location, you will find that what your work means to you will change over time. When you start out, you will naturally want to publish and carry forward the work that began with your dissertation. You will be learning more about teaching and becoming involved in institutional service. Over your initial years, your self-concept of your mix of teaching, research, and service will change. This shift occurs because of the institution(s) you work for, the assignments you receive, your level of success at each component of your mix, and the students you deal with.

248. COMPLETION TIME. No matter how long you think it will take to

- write a paper based on your research,
- see the paper you just submitted in print,
- complete a research project,
- prepare a new course, or
- prepare for a session of a course you gave previously,

it will take longer.

Your estimates of how long each activity will require are influenced by your degree of optimism. In general,

- wide-eyed optimists always think the task will be completed on time,
- mildly realistic optimists think the task will take their estimated time plus 10%, and
- pessimists assume the delay is at least 50% on average.

Corollary: even if you add these delay times to your estimate, it will still take longer than that.

249. FAILURE IS AN OPPORTUNITY. Robert F. Kennedy said, "Forgive your enemies. But remember their names."

Our goal in these hints is to facilitate your success and prevent failure. We wish you the best: that you complete your PhD, secure an appointment, achieve tenure, and in due time are promoted to full professor.

If you fail, try to learn from the experience. Most scholars, including the great world-class ones, experienced one or more failures along the way.

If you fail, say, to achieve tenure the first time, see what you can learn from the experience. Do you need to publish more articles or improve your teaching? Did you find out that one of your colleagues cannot be trusted? Each of these is a valuable lesson.

Try not to become consumed with anger and regret. Regret about yesterday only degrades your own experience today. Enjoy today. Look to the future.

Note

1. Alan Lakein, *How to Get Control of Your Time and Life* (New York: Penguin Signet, 1974).

15

FINAL THOUGHTS

HINT 250: "THE RICH GET RICHER." Once you establish a reputation, people will pursue you.

250. "THE RICH GET RICHER" is a saying that holds true in academia as well as in society in general. Once you establish a reputation, people will pursue you to do things, such as write papers, make presentations at prestigious places, and consult. To reach this position you must earn it. If you do reach it, remember that fame is transitory. You must keep running and doing new things to keep demand for you going. So, once you become one of the powerful 100 (Hint 2), you will gain rewards, but you will also work furiously to keep your riches. Those who read these hints will want to take your place.

251. TREAT STUDENTS AS THOUGH THEY WERE GUESTS IN YOUR HOME. This advice is simple and sound. If you carry nothing else away from these hints, remember this one.

16

CONCLUSION AND ENVOI

PROFESSOR IS THE BEST JOB ON THE PLANET.

N THESE HINTS WE DESCRIBED LIFE based on our own experiences (and mistakes) as well as on observing our colleagues at universities throughout the country. We did not try to quote the many learned studies of academe by academics nor paint a picture of the ideal world that academe should be. For example, we believe, as most aspiring academics do, that teaching should be more respected and rewarded than it is, but we know that in many institutions teaching is a necessary but far from sufficient condition for tenure.

These hints apply in today's academic job market. We hope the coming demographic reversal will provide the impetus to change the system so this book will be read as an artifact of an ancient, more cynical age.

When we started writing these hints, we found previous attempts to encapsulate similar wisdom. In typical academician's fashion, of course, we did not read them. We invite readers to send us their own rules, so we may tell future students about them in future editions.

Envoi

In this book, we are frank, cynical when necessary, and hard-nosed. We provide you with the best career advice we can. We hope this approach does not leave you with a jaundiced view of academia. We consider *professor* to be the best job available on the planet. Universities are wonderful, and occasionally transcendent, places to work. Most, but by no means all, of the great intellectual and scientific advances since the Enlightenment were made in universities. It is a thrill and an honor to contribute to knowledge through your own scholarship. Furthermore, you may well conclude that the most valuable and meaningful work you do is teaching and mentoring students. It is your rare opportunity to guide the expansion and development of young (and older) minds and ideas over your entire lifetime.

Enter this exciting world, but with your eyes wide open.

Appendices

Hint 293: Addictions . . . and **Hint 296:** Meditation

APPENDIX A

Mechanics of the Dissertation

WE PUT OUR THOUGHTS on the mechanics of the dissertation into this appendix because they are of interest for a short but important time: from when you are nearing the end of your first draft until you submit the dissertation to the registrar with the requisite payments. They also serve as a reminder for young faculty asked to serve on PhD committees.

252. ORAL EXAMINATIONS in the PhD process can occur at three points:

- as part of your prelim (or qualifying) examination,
- when you present your dissertation proposal to your faculty committee, and
- when you defend your completed dissertation.

You shouldn't go into such meetings without knowing what the structure will be. In this hint, we present a typical pattern for an oral exam. Find out if this template describes how your department structures its meetings.

When you arrive, the faculty committee chair may ask you to leave the room while the committee discusses how they want to proceed during the meeting.

After you return, you will first be asked to give a brief presentation of your written prelims, proposal, or completed dissertation. Carefully plan a clear, well-organized presentation. Keep it brief. Unless your department requires something different, limit your remarks to 10 or 15 minutes. Sometimes a faculty member will interrupt you to ask a question. Answer it clearly and fully. The time required to answer usually does not count toward your 15 minutes, but find out beforehand if it will.

Next, each professor will ask you, in turn, a series of questions. Answer each to the best of your ability. If you simply don't know an answer, just admit it.

Sometimes one professor will jump in while his or her colleague is questioning you, and the orderly sequence can evaporate. Do not worry if this happens. On rare occasions, two members of your committee will disagree with each other about an issue and start to argue. This is the best of all outcomes from your point of view.

When the questioning is completed, you will be asked to leave the room while the faculty members discuss and assess your presentation and responses.

Then they will call you back into the room and give you their feedback.

253. Visual aids in oral presentations. Should you use a visual aid like PowerPoint (Hint 86) for your presentation? You have three choices:

- present your work verbally without a visual aid,
- use PowerPoint, or
- distribute printouts of your PowerPoint slides.

259. HANDING IN THE DISSERTATION TO THE REGISTRAR. Your institution's registrar uses strict guidelines for the version of the dissertation you hand in, including spacing, table format, bond paper, and reference specifications. Follow those guidelines religiously. Learn them while you are conducting your research, not at the last minute.

If your committee requires one mode of presentation, your decision has been made for you. Otherwise, base your choice on your comfort level. Be as calm and focused as possible during this exam. If you feel that PowerPoint will improve your talk, use it. If you panic when a technological glitch occurs, speak without visual aids or distribute hard copies. (Be aware, though, that your committee members may start to read ahead in the copies and tune out your carefully crafted verbal presentation.) Alternatively, you can plan to use PowerPoint but drop it if there is a technical glitch and distribute the printed version instead.

There is nothing wrong with a simple, clear verbal presentation.

254. WAITING FOR THE COMMITTEE'S DECISION AFTER THE ORAL EXAMINATION. It is natural to be anxious while you are standing in the hall, waiting to learn your committee's decision. Don't panic, even if the committee takes a long time.

Remember that this occasion may be the first time your faculty committee has met as a group to discuss your work. They will undertake a thoughtful, detailed discussion of your work, its strengths, and areas for improvement. Also, we are sorry to report, sometimes professors stray in these discussions to pressing matters of faculty governance or politics, or to the latest movie, and who knows what else.

255. POST–ORAL EXAM REWRITES. Usually the committee requires you to rewrite some of your dissertation after the defense. Don't be surprised, and don't view it as an indication of failure.

The dissertation proposal meeting determines the final shape and design of your dissertation research. Suggested changes can include the research question, how you will proceed, methodology, editorial changes, and additions to the literature review. The faculty believes its recommendation will help you produce a high-quality dissertation. Welcome and incorporate their suggestions—unless you can make a persuasive argument why you should not do so, and they agree. Otherwise, you don't really have a choice.

At the dissertation defense meeting, occasionally you will be asked to conduct an additional analysis. More frequently the faculty will ask for editorial changes. Even if you pass the defense, you have not earned your PhD. You do not finish your graduate studies until you make the changes, and your committee members sign the appropriate pages of the dissertation.

Plan for rewriting time after each examination. Do *not* plan to take a trip right after the defense to celebrate or start a new job. If no edits or changes are required, little will be lost. You will have some postdefense breathing room.

256. FACULTY SIGNATURES. Following each oral examination, faculty members sign the appropriate forms to signify their approval. For prelim orals, the signatures mean you passed.

For a proposal, the signed form signifies your proposal is approved and you are "advanced to candidacy." Signing can occur in one of three ways:

- If no changes are requested, or if the changes are small, the committee members may all sign at the end of the defense.
- If the requested changes are nontrivial, all committee members may wait to sign until the revisions are made.
- In an alternative approach, to streamline the revision process, the chair withholds his or her signature until after your rewrite but the other committee members sign at the end of the meeting.

Typically, for a dissertation defense, three sets of signatures are required:

- The committee signs a form stating you have passed the oral defense.
- Each member of the full committee signs the second page of your dissertation.
- The chair signs the dissertation cover sheet.

The options on timing of signing for the dissertation follow the same pattern as for the proposal.

257. EXTERNAL EXAMINERS. If you have the option to invite an external examiner or reader to your dissertation defense, carefully weigh the advantages and disadvantages.

You can create an opportunity to impress one of the 100 powerful people (Hint 2) with the quality of your work, which can lead to a job offer. Conversely, on rare occasions the external reader decides to impress the committee members, or is simply an SOB, and savagely criticizes your work. Because you certainly don't want this situation, find out as much as you can about a distinguished outsider before sending an invitation. Your faculty mentor (Hint 5) can provide useful information and can help by communicating in advance with the outsider.

258. GUESTS AT YOUR DISSERTATION DEFENSE. In our age of transparency, your dissertation defense is open to whomever shows up. Fellow graduate students nearing their own defense often come to obtain insight into what the defense is about. Some candidates invite friends and family members to the defense. We advise against it. Yes, they provided emotional support as you persisted through graduate school. Yes, you would like to share the culmination of your effort with them. But their presence could be awkward for you and for them if the defense takes a critical, or nasty, turn.

APPENDIX B

Outside Income

PROFESSORS, BEING HUMAN, look to maximize their income no matter how large or small it is. Opportunities exist for earning more from the university through teaching overloads, summer sessions, or executive or noncredit courses, among others. However, most schools treat you for such work the same way they treat adjunct faculty. They pay as little as possible to maximize their income.

This appendix discusses outside income from consulting, grants, and contracts. In Appendix C, we'll talk about other sources of income such as writing textbooks (Hint 273).

260. CONSULTING AS A HIRED HAND. Consulting involves doing work for an organization for compensation, as opposed to your professional activities that contribute to your field but are not compensated. Examples of professional activities include reviewing papers submitted to journals, reviewing grant proposals, and serving on or chairing committees of a national or local professional association. In consulting, you are a hired hand, asked to give advice about what to do. Typically you are paid on a time basis.

261. DON'T LIVE ON YOUR CONSULTING INCOME. Consulting income is found money; it comes to you episodically. Do *not* plan on future consulting income under any circumstances when constructing your family budget. Even if you can trace a steady $5,000 or more per year from consulting over the past six years, you are not guaranteed to earn any consulting income next year unless you have a contract in hand. Even then, corporate fortunes change, and you can be terminated. We recommend you use your consulting income after you receive it to buy large, durable items (a new TV or computer or refrigerator), or to save it for a major vacation, or to buy a house, or to sock it away for your kids' college tuition.

Remember, as a consultant you are running a business, and one of the risks is that you, like a plumber or a house painter, don't always get paid what you and your client agreed on and may not be paid in the agreed-upon time.

262. CONSULTING INCOME IS TAXABLE. Don't go out and spend the consulting checks you receive until you put money aside to pay the taxes on it. Consulting income is like all other income and can put you into a higher tax bracket. Whoever hires you as a consultant has to file a 1099 form, and the IRS is superb in using that form to find you if you don't report the income. Fortunately, you report your consulting income on Schedule C of your tax forms. This schedule allows you to deduct legitimate expenses incurred in generating the income.

263. GRANTS AND CONTRACTS. Receiving an academic salary for nine months' work seems to leave you vast amounts of time to undertake lucrative additional work, such as consulting. It usually does not work out that way. For example, your teaching responsibilities often spill over into summer. More to the point, even if you are a full professor, you may need that summer for research and writing. The best way to earn extra income while moving toward academic goals is to secure grants and contracts. Most federal agencies and other funding organizations that provide research support for summer work usually pay the equivalent of two months' salary (i.e., two ninths of your academic salary). Some may provide three months' support. Some but not all research universities allow faculty to work one day a week during the regular year for pay by outside sources.

264. THE SUMMER TEACHING OPTION. Junior and senior professors alike sometimes slip into doing extensive summer teaching, usually at reduced rates. It is a way to earn needed extra income by doing something you know how to do. You should know that you incur what the economists call an *opportunity cost* associated with this income: you close out other opportunities, especially those in research and writing, that could advance your career. However, if your school offers substantial summer research grants, go for them.

265. HIRE A TAX SPECIALIST TO FILL OUT FORM 1040 because not all outside income is taxed equally. Income on your paycheck from your institution may be taxed differently than income from independent work such as consulting. In brief: as an employee, all income (including regular teaching, overload or summer teaching, summer or other grants) from your institution is treated as regular taxable income. If you are an independent consultant or an author, or run any other kind of business, you can deduct many of the expenses (e.g., computers, travel) associated with these activities from your tax return on Schedule C. When faced with alternative opportunities, compare what you will make in terms of after-tax, not before-tax, amounts.

We strongly recommend you consult a tax specialist about how to prepare your Form 1040 income tax return, particularly Schedule

C. A good tax specialist who knows what can and cannot be deducted will often save you a considerable amount and is worth the investment.

266. PRO BONO WORK. If you are a beginning professor, chances are you are struggling to make ends meet. Later in your career, you should consider doing some consulting jobs pro bono, that is, for free. In the past few years each of us has advised organizations pro bono. For example, we worked pro bono advising a nonprofit conflict resolution and peace organization about how to evaluate its educational activities, advised a religious group in another country about founding a college, and led a team of students in improving an orchestra's database.

267. CONSULTING PAY RATE. If you are being considered for a consulting job, you will be asked what your consulting rate is. Fees for consulting vary by discipline and by client; therefore, it is difficult for us to suggest generic rules that always work. Nonetheless, here is a best practice guideline for your daily rate for business clients:

- Take the annual pay in your nine-month contract and divide it by 165, the standard number of working days in nine months. That calculation gives your daily income from your institution.
- Multiply the number you just computed by 2, because you must be paid more for your knowledge than just your regular pay, and it also takes care of deductions such as Social Security and Medicare taxes.

For example, if your nine-month salary is $66,000, dividing by 165 yields a daily income of $400. Multiplying $400 by 2 results in $800/day ($100/hour) as your consulting rate.

Some additional considerations:

- Charge not-for-profit organizations a lower rate than for-profit groups. They have less money and usually are not able to afford your full rate.
- If you are really a world expert in your field, or if your school's salaries are in the lower quartile of academic salaries, you can of course charge more than the amount computed by the above method.
- If you can, find out what other consultants are charging the firm. It's a delicate question to ask, and some people will inflate their actual rate. Nonetheless, don't be bashful about it. If you ask too much, you lose a client; if you ask too little, you'll kick yourself for it later.
- Should you charge for travel time in addition to travel cost reimbursement? Sometimes you must travel quite a distance to the organization that hired you. It is better to address this issue explicitly when you are negotiating the consulting agreement. We tend not to charge for travel time (but do charge for travel expenses) if we are not working on the client's project while traveling. Some consultants charge half their rate for travel time.

268. WARNING! YOU CAN'T TEACH ELSEWHERE FOR OUTSIDE MONEY if you are on the tenure track. Universities and colleges generally do not let you moonlight at another school without permission. It's a conflict of interest. The specific permission rules vary from place to place, but every institution has them. We know of one case where a tenured faculty member in an eastern U.S. university took a second appointment in another university within driving distance. When found out, he was asked to resign by both, and he did.

APPENDIX C

How to Become a Millionaire

N THIS APPENDIX WE DISCUSS several strategies that could make you wealthy. Your university salary is barely enough if you must feed your family and repay your college debts. Achieving wealth with these strategies is quite rare. Unlike all the other hints in this book, the ones that follow in this appendix introduce risk that can *damage*, if not *destroy*, your academic career rather than improve it.

This appendix is largely tongue in cheek. It's a long shot, but you can become wealthy as an academic. For example, a specialist in operations research, a tenured full professor at the University of British Columbia, developed a successful system to beat the odds at the race track. His betting advice appeared in the Daily Racing Form under the pseudonym "Dr. Z."[1]

We have worked with academic researchers who were billionaires, but they earned their money the old-fashioned way—they inherited it. Most of us, however, chose academia because we are motivated by other goals and values.

269. MAKING (OR NOT MAKING) A FORTUNE THROUGH PUBLISHING AND PUBLIC APPEARANCES. As a professor, you have (or can create) opportunities for making money beyond your university or college pay. For some opportunities, people will come to you and clamor for your services, while, for other opportunities, you will need to go out and solicit clients. Here are some opportunities categorized by their potentially (but not certain) large payoffs:

- writing textbooks (see Hints 223, 273, and 274), but pay attention to the caveats in the hints
- writing popular nonfiction (e.g., history, public policy) or fiction
- performing in public (if you are a musician, singer, actor, or lecturer)
- consulting in industry or government
- owning or running a business on the side
- being a professional expert witness
- serving on a board of directors

Opportunities that have almost certainly small payoffs are

- writing op-ed pieces for newspapers
- serving as a proposal reviewer for government research agencies or book publishers
- honoraria, such as for editing a journal
- appearing on television as an expert
- writing books, such as the one you're reading, for small or impoverished audiences

Be aware, however, that these opportunities take away some of your valuable time professionally and personally. They don't help you achieve tenure or promotion, and they can generate jealousies that affect your career negatively (Hint 223). If the payoff proves to be small, you will often wind up working for less than minimum wage. On the other hand, if you rake in enough, you can quit your professorship and live off the profits.

270. WRITE A BEST-SELLING NOVEL. Consider Erich Segal. He was launched on a promising academic career as a tenure-track professor in classics at Yale. He came to Yale with bachelor's (with honors), master's, and PhD degrees from Harvard where he served as class poet and Latin orator.

In 1970 he wrote a romantic novel, *Love Story,* set at Harvard. This book was an enormous best seller, although the critics did not consider it great literature. One wrote, "It skips from cliche to cliche with an abandon that would chill even the blood of a True Romance editor."[2] Nonetheless, there were 21 printings in the first 12 months, and the initial paperback printing was 4.3 million copies.[3] He wrote the screenplay for the movie, which grossed $200 million and was credited for saving Paramount Studios from bankruptcy. Segal became an international celebrity and later worked with John Lennon on the screenplay for *Yellow Submarine.*

Segal was denied tenure at Yale in 1972. Moral: don't make your tenure reviewers jealous.

271. YOU MAY WANT TO USE A PSEUDONYM FOR NONACADEMIC PUBLICATIONS. If you are convinced your novel will be a blockbuster, consider using a pseudonym. For example, the late Carolyn Gold Heilbrun was the Avalon Foundation Professor in the humanities and the first woman tenured in Columbia University's English department. Although she published a number of highly regarded academic books, she also published a successful series of novels as Amanda Cross.

Pseudonyms are frequently employed by professionals whose writing might conflict with the norms or expectations of their day jobs.

272. START YOUR OWN CONSULTING FIRM. Once you have your degree, consider expanding your consulting activities by launching a consulting firm. If the firm is successful and grows, you may find yourself running a multimillion-dollar organization. Needless to say, you need professional knowledge of your consulting discipline, salesmanship, proposal writing skills, management expertise, and a good deal of luck.

Two striking success stories are those of Abt Associates, started by Dr. Clark Abt in 1965, and the Cosmos Corporation, started by Robert Yin in 1980. Each now is a substantial successful firm. Abt Associates has described itself as "a mild-mannered social reform organization, an informal graduate school, and a profit-making company."[4]

273. WRITE A COLLEGE TEXTBOOK. It's possible to become wealthy by writing a textbook. If you produce a good, clear textbook, especially for a course offered in most colleges and universities, the royalties are substantial, especially if new students will be taking that course year after year.

However, there are some drawbacks.

1. It will probably damage your academic career (Hint 223), although there are exceptions. Paul Samuelson and Paul Krugman each won the Nobel Prize in economics and wrote leading introductory economics textbooks.
2. Other people will have had the same idea; the competition is considerable.
3. In rapidly changing fields, your book will quickly become outdated. Even in slowly changing fields, you will need to revise your textbook from time to time.
4. Writing a textbook usually is like teaching an introductory course. You are not building greater knowledge or a greater reputation in your specialty (Hint 6).

Sometimes publishers take a chance on your book if you can guarantee sales in your own courses over the next three or four years. With luck, the book will take off and become a standard.

274. WRITE A TEXTBOOK FOR K–12 EDUCATION. If successful, a K–12 text could be more lucrative than winning the lottery. In many states, textbooks are adopted for all students in a given grade. Should your book be adopted by a state, hopefully a populous one, the guaranteed sales are enormous.

However, you are entering a world of complex, byzantine maneuvering and competition. Major textbook publishers are powerful, and for minor publishers it's tough sledding competing with them.

275. WRITE A CROSSOVER BOOK. Professors build their reputations by publishing articles and books in their specialties. Almost always, their only readers are other professors, graduate students, and their own families. Sometimes, however, a faculty member produces a successful crossover book, a work that is respected and receives laudatory reviews from his or her academic colleagues while also selling well with the general public.

Such books are difficult to write, however. If your book is to fly off the shelves at Barnes and Noble, it has to be readable and entertaining. Few people reach the level of clear and creative writing that is required for that. Furthermore, even among highly skilled professional nonfiction writers, *New York Times* best sellers are rare.

Nonetheless, some university scholars have written best sellers, including Peter Drucker, Margaret Mead, Paul Krugman, Gail Kearns Goodwin, and Stephen Hawking.

We believe that professors who produce crossover books perform a valuable public service. However, remember Hint 270: unless you become a world-class public intellectual like the people in the preceding paragraph, you may be denigrated by your academic peers as a mere popularizer. Here is a false equation that does not work mathematically, but still describes the behavior of many misguided professors: excellent technical productivity plus commercial success is respected less than excellent technical productivity alone.

276. SAVE IN A TIAA–CREF OR OTHER ANNUITY PLAN. If you are risk averse (Hint 137), you will likely judge each of the previous approaches as too dependent on luck for you to attempt. The recession that started in 2007 highlighted the risk of speculating in stocks or bonds. If you are a really risk-averse person, consider the retirement plan offered by your institution to determine whether the result is a million-dollar nest egg. When combined with Social Security, the result could be a payout of about $100,000 per year before taxes.

If your institution belongs to TIAA–CREF, which is the portable 403(b) retirement plan offered by most colleges and universities (Hint 142), you can wind up accumulating the million in cash from the combination of your employer's and your own tax-deferred contributions.

Corollary: many of the retirement systems for state universities and colleges guarantee an annuity based on your three highest years of salary. These annuities can also create large payouts.

Bottom line: if you plan to stay in academia, you can become a millionaire through an annuity, but you have to wait until retirement to cash in.

Notes

1. Dr. Z noticed that the odds displayed at the track are based only on win bets; place bets often followed a different pattern. He advised that income could be made by capitalizing on this discrepancy.

2. M. Fox, Obituary of Erich Segal, *New York Times*, January 19, 2010.

3. E. Woo, Obituary of Erich Segal, *Los Angeles Times*, January 20, 2010.

4. http://www.abtassociates.com/page.cfm?PageID = 104.

APPENDIX D

Writing Hints

THIS APPENDIX EXPANDS on Hint 213. It contains tips that will help you in writing and editing your manuscripts, whether they are your dissertation, papers, books, or monographs. These tips are based on our experiences. Furthermore, one of us spent eight years of his youth as a technical editor. As implied in Hints 212 and 213, good writing increases the odds that your submission will be accepted.

We use the term *paper* in what follows to represent all forms of publication. You may find that specific journals and publishers have idiosyncrasies of their own. If so, follow them rather than us.

277. EXPLAIN ONLY WHAT THE READER NEEDS TO KNOW. Don't try to explain your field or subfield from first principles. You are not writing a textbook for undergraduates or an article for your alumni magazine. You can assume that your reader is familiar with the field in general and knows all that. Do explain what the reader needs to know to understand what you are saying.

278. AVOID PASSIVE VOICE. Passive voice is dull and pedantic. Typically, in passive voice, you use the verb first and then the subject.

Active voice makes your work more interesting to read. In active voice, the subject performs the action given in the verb, such as in the following:

> Passive voice: The girl was bitten by the dog.
> Active voice: The dog bit the girl.
> Passive voice: Statistical tests were conducted to check the validity of the hypothesis.
> Active voice: Statistical tests checked the validity of the hypothesis.

279. AVOID *SHOULD* AND *MUST*. These prescriptive words assume you are in a position to give advice and that you found the only way to do something. This case is rare. Authors of business and policy papers are particularly fond of this bad habit, although it also shows up in many other fields.

280. AVOID USING TOO MUCH BOLDFACE AND ITALICS. You SHOUT when you use **bold** or *italics* in your text. Bold and italics used sparingly are a great help when you present something important, but if you use them over and over, the reader starts ignoring them. Italics used the first time you define a term is OK. Similarly, you can put a term in quotation marks when you first use it.

281. YOU CAN RARELY BE BOTH *EFFECTIVE* AND *EFFICIENT*. Some people use these words together almost as if they were a single word. Rarely can you achieve both simultaneously; usually the best you can do is trade one for the other.

282. AVOID GENERALIZING FROM A SINGLE CASE. You are limited to the results from that case and that case alone.

283. DON'T BE AFRAID TO USE NUMBERED OR BULLETED LISTS. Don't try to put everything into straight text, otherwise you might wind up writing something that looks like

> A method . . .
> Another method . . .
> Another method . . .
> A fourth method . . .

It is better to say:

The methods are:

> 1. . . .
> 2. . . .
> 3. . . .
> 4. . . .

Because a list breaks material up visually, it helps your reader follow you more easily.

284. Use figures and tables. Like lists, figures and tables break up the monotony of text. They make information easier to read and understand. Almost all word processing programs include capabilities that let you create tables and draw simple figures.

285. Learn to use styles in word processing programs. Microsoft Word and most other text programs contain features that make it easy to create different-looking documents. The journal you write a paper for will specify what format they want for submissions. Styles, built into the word processor, let you change the appearance of the document automatically to fit your requirements.

286. Use the spell-checker. Papers with spelling errors are often rejected out of hand. They show that you are either careless or illiterate, neither of which are desirable traits. Use your software's spell-checker on the final draft. Be careful, however. Often, you can misspell a word and the spell-checker accepts it. For example, if you type *their* when you meant to type *there*, the spell-checker won't show it as an error.

After you run the spell-checker and make corrections, be sure to read the paper one more time from end to end (better still, ask someone else to read it as well) before you send it out.

287. PAY SPECIAL ATTENTION TO REFERENCES. Your paper's reviewers and your readers will read your in-text citations and turn to the list of references. Use the following tips:

1. Be sure your references are accurate in name spellings, dates of publication, journal name or publisher, and other details. Remember, an author of one of your references may review your paper. Think about the retribution if you spell the author's name wrong.

2. Provide a source for all quotations. If you quote someone or some source, be sure to include a reference with full publishing information. If you don't, you can be accused of plagiarism.

3. Use multiple references when you synthesize several sources. Be sure to include references for all the sources you use.

4. Be sure each URL has a date.[1] It is OK these days to use electronic publications as sources. If you can't find an author's name, start with the document's title. Exception: quotations your source designates as being anonymous use *anonymous*. Use n.d. (no date) if a date is not available. A few journals still ask you to include the date when you last accessed the Web reference.

5. Compile a list of references at the end of your paper.
   Exception 1: some journals require references in footnotes.
   Exception 2: book publishers sometimes use references in endnotes.

6. When using an in-text citation, follow the style requirements of the journal or book publisher. Some examples:
"The results (Smith 1998; Smith and Jones 2004) . . .²"
"As shown by Jones (2006) . . ."
Refer to one of several references by the same author in the same year by adding a, b, c, and so on to the year: (Smith, 2004b).

288. ELIMINATE POOR WRITING HABITS. For example,

1. avoid "there are" particularly at the start of a sentence.
Replace: There are three ways to obtain knowledge, . . .
With: Three ways to obtain knowledge are . . .
2. don't split infinitives by putting one or more words between *to* and the verb. You can always write your way around a split infinitive.
Replace: To successfully manage knowledge, . . .
With: To manage knowledge successfully, . . .
3. do not use "etc." The reader does not know what you include in your *et cetera*. Readers often interpret "etc." differently than you do. You can convey the same idea by using "including" or "such as."
Replace: . . . text, voice, graphics, etc.
With: . . . including text, voice, and graphics.
4. use "to" instead of "in order to." In most cases, particularly at the beginning of paragraphs, "to" is sufficient. You need "in order to" only when you mean "for the purpose of."
Replace: In order to obtain knowledge, . . .
With: To obtain knowledge, . . .

289. BAD WORDS refers to words that cause the reader difficulty rather than words banned by the Federal Communications Commission. Words listed in the first column of Table D.1 are best

TABLE D.1
Bad Words

Word(s) to Avoid	Reason
Cutting-edge	Cliché
Comprise	*Comprise* is used correctly when you say the whole comprises, or is *comprised of*, the parts (e.g., The Union comprises 50 states), but incorrectly if you say the parts comprise the whole (e.g., Fifty states constitute [or *make up* or *compose*] the Union, rather than *comprise* it).
Discovered	Usually you mean to say *found* or *obtained*. Discovery implies scientific discovery, or when the known world was smaller, finding a previously unknown territory.
Dramatically	It's meaningless hyperbole. Do you mean a Noh play in which little happens, or a melodrama?
Finally	Not needed at the beginning of a sentence or as the last item in a list. The reader can tell from the context that it is the end.
Ideal	*Ideal* means "absolute perfection" and is unprovable.
Incredible	Hyperbole
It is important	Let the reader find out that something is important.
Perfect	Hyperbole. You can rarely prove perfection.
Perfect solution	Advertising hyperbole
Recent	Academic writing is read for many years after publication. Something published in 2007 is recent in 2008 but not in 2012.
This	When used alone, the antecedent of "this" is not clear. For example, "This proves the hypothesis" should be replaced by "This analysis proves the hypothesis."
Utilize	*Utilize* is not a synonym for the verb "use." *Utilize* means "to make use of" and sounds pretentious.

avoided. The second column explains why. The words are representative. In general, if a word is a cliché or hyperbole or advertising or pretentious, replace it with a simpler word that conveys your meaning.

Notes

1. *URL* stands for "universal resource locator." It refers to the address of the resource on the Internet.

2. Some journals, such as those that follow American Psychological Association (APA) style, use the ampersand (&) rather than "and."

APPENDIX E

Your Health

YOU MUST STAY HEALTHY to continue to hold down the academic job you sought for so long. Unless you keep your health, you can become ill, fatigue easily, or see your body decay. You can't guard against all health hazards (and you may inherit some from your family), but you can do some relatively simple things to maintain your health and stay ahead of your competitors. In this appendix, we offer hints about some of the problems you can encounter and what you can do to maintain balance and health. These hints are based on our experiences. They are not intended as medical advice. We are neither physicians nor health specialists.

290. AVOID STRESS. Although we go into academia because we think it involves little stress, that's a legend that is not true. If you're junior and nontenured, you can expect that obtaining tenure will be the most intense, stressful experience you will face in your entire career. You will be wondering whether you will be awarded tenure (it is never a slam dunk!). You will worry about what you will do if you aren't. Furthermore, stress is not necessarily over once you become tenured, although it is usually diminished. Of course, if you are a type A personality (impatient, insecure about yourself, competitive, aggressive, and rarely relax) you add your own internal stress to all the rest.

Stress caused by the following also awaits you from outside academe:

- Money. For most professors, unless you or your family are really well off when you start your academic career, you will face the problem of managing much more salary than you ever had as a graduate student. Although the salary may seem princely, you will still need to pay off your student debts, and you will make considerably less than senior professors. The monthly check may never seem to go far enough. You must learn how to manage your money.
- Family responsibilities. Most people receive their PhDs between the ages of 25 and 35. If you don't already have a spouse or partner, these are often the years when you take on family responsibilities, emotional and financial, in addition to your nontrivial workload.
- Parents. As people live longer, your parents and grandparents will need care, and the responsibilities for that care can become yours.

The problems of money, family responsibilities, and parents don't go away even after tenure. Whether you are tenured or not, you will experience stress from within your institution. For example, a bad dean, a school in financial crisis, a department riven by politics, and outside political attacks on the university all contribute to stress. You will also feel transient stresses, such as the potential repercussions from a student you failed or from the rejection of a paper you thought was great.

291. START A HEALTH AND FITNESS PROGRAM if you are not already involved in one. As academics, we take the written word seriously.

Therefore, we suggest you begin by reading one or two of the many excellent books about health. Use well-established books, rather than the latest faddish one on magic exercises or fantastic diets. Talk with people in your school's health service or athletic department for specific recommendations.

292. EXERCISE. The establishment (public health officials and the medical community) is always after us to exercise regularly. The establishment is right. If you're a couch potato who goes from the computer to the television and then to bed, find a half hour every day for some form of exercise, preferably aerobic.[1] For example,

- walk a half hour every day,
- ride a bike,
- jog, or
- swim.

If you enjoy a form of exercise, you are most likely to continue and make it a lifelong habit. If you prefer, or you need to stay disciplined, use a gym. Often, institutions offer exercise programs for faculty.

293. ADDICTIONS. We discuss three addictions here: smoking, drugs, and alcohol. This information also applies to other addictions, such as gambling or being an e-mail junkie.

STOP smoking immediately. We know this is easier for us to say than for you to do.

Many stop-smoking programs are available. Shop around until you find a program that works for you. The cost of the cigarettes you don't smoke will more than pay for the program.

Drugs and alcohol. We won't go into detail on drugs or alcohol here. Suffice it to say that if you are addicted to either or both, it can

- be successful grounds for firing you even if you are tenured. Obtaining another appointment will be difficult.
- reduce your research output, particularly for tenure.
- be nearly impossible to hide for long periods of time. You're a public person (Hint 152) who is observed by all around you. Some of your students or colleagues will pick up on it, and word will get around.

294. WEIGHT CONTROL. Being overweight is the biggest factor above and beyond smoking that contributes to illness, fatigue, and decay. Obesity and even less extreme forms of being overweight lead to scary outcomes: high blood pressure, diabetes, sleep apnea, and some forms of cancer, to name just a few. Bookstores and libraries are filled with diet books and programs, from the Scarsdale Diet to Atkins to Jenny Craig. Unfortunately, many of these diets are fads, and a lot of them aren't even effective. You are more likely to achieve weight loss over the long term if you follow a healthy diet and exercise regularly.

295. DIET. Studies of people who live to be quite old (including those over 100) consistently find common diet elements. Diet recommendations could easily yield a book much larger than this one. Read one or two books on healthy nutrition. It is a complex subject and there is much to learn—for example, the importance and the different kinds of omega-3 fatty acids. The following are some of the consistent recommendations from the epidemiological, public health, and medical literatures:

- Eat a variety of fruits and vegetables.
- Limit your intake of red meat.

- Make sure you eat adequate amounts of protein.
- Eat nuts, beans, and whole-grain bread.
- Limit your intake of complex and refined carbohydrates, for example, potatoes, pasta, rice, bread, and needless to say, cookies, candy, and soda.
- Drink plenty of water.

If your health plan pays for it (and even if it doesn't), it is helpful to consult a professional dietician occasionally.

296. MEDITATION. When we suggest meditation, we are not talking about a bearded man sitting cross-legged in front of a cave or high on a mountaintop. Male or female, you can meditate anywhere, and it's not complicated. Do it for at least 10 minutes a day.

Why meditate? The medical literature increasingly highlights the cognitive, physical, and emotional benefits of meditation.

To meditate, simply sit in a quiet room, breathe slowly and deeply, and try not to obsess about your worries or the tasks on your to-do list. To drive such thoughts out of your mind while meditating, you will find it helpful to use a mantra, which is a constantly repeated phrase.

297. ACUPUNCTURE. One of us benefited greatly from acupuncture. This treatment is not a fad. Chinese medicine, including acupuncture, is about 5,000 years old. Acupuncture is used successfully to treat pain, hypertension, insulin/blood sugar balance, and many other ailments.

We suggest using acupuncture as a complement rather than a replacement for traditional Western medicine. Finding an excellent acupuncture specialist can be challenging. But, then, finding an excellent cardiologist can also be challenging.

After taking a detailed medical history, the acupuncturist places small needles at just the right spots to combat your ailments as you lie on your back. You will continue to lie there for about 45 minutes once the needles are inserted. Placement of the needles is based on a theory about the flow of vital energy, or *chi*, within your body.

The small needles inserted into your body are quite thin and don't hurt, at least not when one of us tried it. However, you may sometimes feel a slight pinching sensation.

298. PHYSICAL APPEARANCE. How you look and interact is observed continually (Hint 152). Fortunately, you're not expected to come to class dressed in a suit as though you were in a 1930s movie. You are, however, expected by your students and by your colleagues to be neat, not disheveled. For young faculty, it helps distinguish you from the students. It also helps if you are thought of as a person who smiles, not frowns.

As you age, your appearance will be affected by your health. For example, as a person involved with books, computers, and student papers, you depend on your vision for your livelihood. It's not shameful for an academic to use glasses (or contacts) rather than squinting. As you head into middle age, you will inevitably become farsighted. Don't do as one colleague we know and keep pushing menus farther and farther away from your face. Buy some reading glasses (even if you purchase them at the local drugstore).

Hearing is lost a little at a time. For males in particular the high frequencies are the first to go. If you've spent a lot of time at rock concerts or at shooting ranges, your hearing has likely been affected, and the symptoms will show up in class. For example, you might find yourself asking students (particularly those who speak softly) to repeat what they said more loudly "so everyone can hear." What's really going on is that you have trouble hearing, and you're becoming less effective in class. Sometimes hearing loss results in poorer teaching ratings. Using hearing aids is not a disgrace.

299. HEALTH AND LIFE INSURANCE. When we wrote this hint in mid-2011, most colleges and universities offered health insurance to their full-time faculty as a fringe benefit.[2] It's almost always a better deal than insurance policies you buy on your own. Yes, in the first years out of graduate school, you'll use health insurance a lot less than your older colleagues, and it may seem like a bad deal. Furthermore, in many cases, adding your spouse and kids to your policy will cost you more than your own insurance, sometimes a lot more. If you're married with a working spouse who is also eligible for health insurance, take the coverage from the plan that is lower in cost. However, premiums by themselves are not an indicator of the best plan. For example, different plans involve different copayments you make every time you use the insurance. Study what is offered and then make a choice. Under no circumstances should you remain without coverage. A serious health disaster can wipe out you and your family financially.

Your institution may offer a minimum amount of life insurance at little or no cost. If it's free, certainly take it. If the cost is minimal, think hard about it (but check the cost against commercial term policies which may cost less). If you're the main breadwinner or a parent, even a little life insurance will be a great help if you get hit by a car crossing the street.

Notes

1. According to the *Oxford English Dictionary*, *aero* is from the Greek meaning "air" and *bic* is from the Greek word *bios* meaning "life." The benefits of aerobics include reduced stress, weight control, improved cardiovascular and muscular fitness, increased flexibility, lower cholesterol, and improved sleep patterns.

2. If you're an adjunct, you probably aren't eligible for health insurance or life insurance. Although you may not be able to get an increase in the pittance that adjuncts are paid because the rates are uniform across the department or the college, you may be able to negotiate some form of health insurance. Try it.

ABOUT THE AUTHORS

DAVID E. DREW and PAUL GRAY (the order of the names under the title was chosen by the flip of a coin) are professor of education and professor of information science at Claremont Graduate University in Claremont, California. You can find out more about them by going to www.cgu.edu/pages/388.asp and to www.cgu.edu/pages/2237.asp.

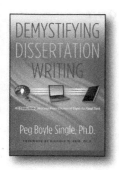

Demystifying Dissertation Writing
A Streamlined Process from Choice of Topic to Final Text
Peg Boyle Single
Foreword by Richard M. Reis

"Whether you're inching towards a dissertation topic, choosing an adviser or already coping with the last stage of doctoral work, this book will be a life-saver. *Demystifying Dissertation Writing* is for anyone who wants to increase their writing productivity and especially for those who experience anxiety, blocking, impatience, perfectionism, or procrastination when they write. Through easy-to-follow steps, Single helps you rise above all these barriers and become a fluent writer."—*JoAnn Moody, Faculty Development and Diversity Specialist,* www.diversityoncampus.com and author of *Faculty Diversity: Problems and Solutions.*

Research shows that five strategies correlate with the successful completion of a dissertation:

- Establishing a consistent writing routine
- Working with a support group
- Consulting your adviser
- Understanding your committee's expectations
- Setting a realistic and timely schedule

Building on these insights, this book is for anyone who needs help in preparing for, organizing, planning, scheduling, and writing the longest sustained writing project they have encountered, particularly if he or she is not receiving sufficient guidance about the process, but also for anyone looking to boost his or her writing productivity.

This book is intended for graduate students and their advisers in the social sciences, the humanities, and professional fields. It can further serve as a textbook for either informal writing groups led by students or for formal writing seminars offered by departments or graduate colleges. The techniques described will help new faculty advise their students more effectively, and even achieve greater fluency in their own writing.

Sty/us

22883 Quicksilver Drive
Sterling, VA 20166-2102

Subscribe to our e-mail alerts: www.Styluspub.com

Advice on Managing Your Career . . . and Beyond

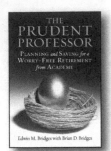

The Prudent Professor
Planning and Saving for a Worry-Free Retirement from Academe
Edwin M. Bridges and Brian D. Bridges

"This is a great read on a tough topic. The writing is simple, direct, and persuasive. The tone is conversational. The examples are clear, and thorny problems are discussed in a straightforward manner. Ed Bridges clarifies all of the issues in a patient way that left me wishing I had this book a decade ago."—***William G. Tierney,*** *University Professor and Director, Center for Higher Education Policy Analysis, University of Southern California*

"Bottom Line: Do I wish I had this book early in my academic career and at the beginning of my retirement? Absolutely! Should those who have thus far ignored retirement planning study its contents and then act? You bet!"—***Stan "Economic Man,"*** *Morningstar Forum*

"An incredibly helpful guide to investment success. Targeted to members of the academic community, the book draws on his own careful research and long personal experience in building—and protecting—his retirement funds. His blunt appraisals of working with TIAA–CREF and with Vanguard (I should know!) are invaluable, indeed priceless."—***John C. Bogle,*** *Founder, The Vanguard Group*

Whether you are a newly minted PhD landing your first job, at mid-career, or even already retired and concerned about how long your money might last, Ed Bridges offers you a straightforward, easy-to-grasp, and structured way to think about money, learn how it works, understand the priorities for your stage in life, determine your objectives, and develop a personal plan most likely to achieve them.

Why a book specifically for those who work in higher education? The chances are that your retirement funds are mostly invested in TIAA–CREF funds, and that the plans created by the different institutions where you have worked, or will work, impose sometimes conflicting limitations of how you can manage your retirement money. This is potentially complex terrain with which many professional financial advisors are unfamiliar.

Pitch Perfect
Communicating with Traditional and Social Media for Scholars,
Researchers, and Academic Leaders
William Tyson
Foreword by Robert Zemsky

"As an academic publisher, I work with hundreds of scholars, encouraging them to communicate their research to the widest audience possible. Each of our authors stands to benefit greatly from Bill Tyson's book, which explains to scholars how they can best share their findings without dumbing down their message. With clear examples and telling anecdotes from across the academic disciplines, Tyson gives faculty a map for transcending their circle of peers and spreading the key points of their research to a larger public."—***Marlie Wasserman,*** *Director, Rutgers University Press*

This book is intended for scholars, researchers, and academic leaders who have a passion to share their knowledge outside their classroom, laboratory, or institution; who want to make a difference; and who believe that the information they possess and ideas they offer are important for a wider public. *Pitch Perfect* is a practical guide to communicating your knowledge and research to broader audiences.

How do you get yourself heard amid the volume of news and information in today's 24-hour news cycle, and get your message across in an environment where blogs and Twitter vie with traditional media? To break through, you need to amplify your ideas and make them relevant for a wider public audience. Bill Tyson—who has been successfully advising scholars and academic leaders on media relations for over 30 years—shows you how.

If your committee requires one mode of presentation, your decision has been made for you. Otherwise, base your choice on your comfort level. Be as calm and focused as possible during this exam. If you feel that PowerPoint will improve your talk, use it. If you panic when a technological glitch occurs, speak without visual aids or distribute hard copies. (Be aware, though, that your committee members may start to read ahead in the copies and tune out your carefully crafted verbal presentation.) Alternatively, you can plan to use PowerPoint but drop it if there is a technical glitch and distribute the printed version instead.

There is nothing wrong with a simple, clear verbal presentation.

254. Waiting for the committee's decision after the oral examination. It is natural to be anxious while you are standing in the hall, waiting to learn your committee's decision. Don't panic, even if the committee takes a long time.

Remember that this occasion may be the first time your faculty committee has met as a group to discuss your work. They will undertake a thoughtful, detailed discussion of your work, its strengths, and areas for improvement. Also, we are sorry to report, sometimes professors stray in these discussions to pressing matters of faculty governance or politics, or to the latest movie, and who knows what else.

255. Post–oral exam rewrites. Usually the committee requires you to rewrite some of your dissertation after the defense. Don't be surprised, and don't view it as an indication of failure.

The dissertation proposal meeting determines the final shape and design of your dissertation research. Suggested changes can include the research question, how you will proceed, methodology, editorial changes, and additions to the literature review. The faculty believes its recommendation will help you produce a high-quality dissertation. Welcome and incorporate their suggestions—unless you can make a persuasive argument why you should not do so, and they agree. Otherwise, you don't really have a choice.

At the dissertation defense meeting, occasionally you will be asked to conduct an additional analysis. More frequently the faculty will ask for editorial changes. Even if you pass the defense, you have not earned your PhD. You do not finish your graduate studies until you make the changes, and your committee members sign the appropriate pages of the dissertation.

Plan for rewriting time after each examination. Do *not* plan to take a trip right after the defense to celebrate or start a new job. If no edits or changes are required, little will be lost. You will have some postdefense breathing room.

256. Faculty signatures. Following each oral examination, faculty members sign the appropriate forms to signify their approval. For prelim orals, the signatures mean you passed.

For a proposal, the signed form signifies your proposal is approved and you are "advanced to candidacy." Signing can occur in one of three ways:

- If no changes are requested, or if the changes are small, the committee members may all sign at the end of the defense.
- If the requested changes are nontrivial, all committee members may wait to sign until the revisions are made.
- In an alternative approach, to streamline the revision process, the chair withholds his or her signature until after your rewrite but the other committee members sign at the end of the meeting.

Typically, for a dissertation defense, three sets of signatures are required:

- The committee signs a form stating you have passed the oral defense.
- Each member of the full committee signs the second page of your dissertation.
- The chair signs the dissertation cover sheet.

The options on timing of signing for the dissertation follow the same pattern as for the proposal.

257. EXTERNAL EXAMINERS. If you have the option to invite an external examiner or reader to your dissertation defense, carefully weigh the advantages and disadvantages.

You can create an opportunity to impress one of the 100 powerful people (Hint 2) with the quality of your work, which can lead to a job offer. Conversely, on rare occasions the external reader decides to impress the committee members, or is simply an SOB, and savagely criticizes your work. Because you certainly don't want this situation, find out as much as you can about a distinguished outsider before sending an invitation. Your faculty mentor (Hint 5) can provide useful information and can help by communicating in advance with the outsider.

258. GUESTS AT YOUR DISSERTATION DEFENSE. In our age of transparency, your dissertation defense is open to whomever shows up. Fellow graduate students nearing their own defense often come to obtain insight into what the defense is about. Some candidates invite friends and family members to the defense. We advise against it. Yes, they provided emotional support as you persisted through graduate school. Yes, you would like to share the culmination of your effort with them. But their presence could be awkward for you and for them if the defense takes a critical, or nasty, turn.

259. HANDING IN THE DISSERTATION TO THE REGISTRAR. Your institution's registrar uses strict guidelines for the version of the dissertation you hand in, including spacing, table format, bond paper, and reference specifications. Follow those guidelines religiously. Learn them while you are conducting your research, not at the last minute.